VOLATILE
WHEN
MIXED

VOLATILE WHEN MIXED
A Collection of Poetry and Prose
Copyright © 2016 LUW Press

ISBN: 978-0-9882367-4-5

Cover design by Lauren Makena and Shai Ashlin

"To every thing there is a season, and a time to every purpose under the heaven…A time to weep, and a time to laugh; a time to mourn, and a time to dance."

-Ecclesiastes 3:1, 4

CONTENTS

CLEANING SPREE

Felicia Rose

Leaves from a windstorm
dally on the porch screen.
Ashes from the stone hearth
idle on the floor.

Hasten, I tell myself,
toil now to spare
tomorrow's self
these never-ending chores.

But I, the present I,
linger in the attic
sweeping cobwebs
from thoughts neglected and obscured.

Nestled on a hassock, I sort through words,
whole cedar trunks of them.
Which shall I keep and which discard?
How shall I arrange them trim and trig?

Ah, there's one I may use
sesquipedalian –
bequeathed years ago
by a dear old friend.

I turn it in my hands
a lexical gem
though surely as cumbrous
as a bucket of steel.
Tucked in the corner charming baskets wrought

of fixed forms and rhyme.
Perfect for petticoats or picnics
but too worn to hold the weight
of ideas.

Joy of joys. Here beneath the floorboards
a jewel box brims with crystal beads
of morphemes. Golden strands
of syntax. Phonemes silent
for far too long.

I unpack these treasures
and polish each one. Then I work
them together
and hang them

from the rafters
so that when the next draft comes along
a tidy grammar
will chime
through the house.

FIVE MINUTES

Dustin Earl

With the glimpse of flowering blossoms rustling in an April breeze or the orange beams of a sunset on wispy clouds, there are times when I catch a glimmer of beauty that stays with me forever. This is why I climb mountains. Only where earth meets sky, can I truly feel free, if for only five minutes.

In the summer of 2008, I arrived in Japan fresh out of college and ready to show the world what I could do. I planned to climb Mt. Fuji as a grand welcoming to the land of the rising sun. Conquering Fuji-san was like conquering myself, proof that I could endure my years away from home.

Unlike the other mountains I've climbed, Mt. Fuji rises so prominently over packed cities and mountainous landscape that it dominates the skyline for more than a hundred miles. It is the subject of countless poems, photographs and artwork, and it is the single most recognizable symbol of Japan.

The best peaks offer more than just a good view; they offer an array of life, nature, and landscape. The trail up Mt. Naomi in Northern Utah passes through meadows thick with wildflowers that slope into an alpine wilderness. Teewinot in the Wyoming Tetons is not for the faint of heart, with its steep trails and dangerous cliffs, rising to a pinnacle that drops a sheer three thousand feet into Cascade Canyon.

Mt. Fuji, an active volcano, offers rocks. Big rocks, small rocks, round rocks, sharp rocks, lots and lots of boring brown rocks.

To be fair, I only climbed the upper part of Fuji-san. A lush landscape surrounds the lower half, but that isn't where people usually start, and like most people, I began my ascent just below tree line at the Subaru Fifth Station on the Yoshida trail, *Yoshida Subaru Gogome*.

The fifth station is a tourist trap, and with the exception of a small Shinto shrine, the hotels and shops looked like a tacky alpine village. If I didn't know any better, I'd have sworn I was in a ski resort.

Mt. Fuji itself looms over the hotels and souvenir shops, or so I imagined, were it not for the clouds blocking the view. Fuji-san is an extraordinarily shy mountain. She's so large she has her own weather patterns and gladly snatches nearby clouds to wrap around herself like a fluffy blanket.

Every good hike needs a walking stick, and with my favorites still back in the U.S., I perused the shops whose selections included a variety of staffs, each with intricately carved mountain gods or local animals. I opted for a plain, four-foot wooden pole. This has since become one of my best hiking sticks.

Two Japanese signs marked the trailhead on the far side of the fifth station, and a line of haggard returning hikers ambled past as I took my first steps onto the trail. They leaned on their own walking sticks, cringing with each step. I gulped and sped on, the path couldn't be *that* difficult, could it?

Lush trees and pink flowers lined the way, and the hum of cicada song punctuated the ambiance. Miniature shrines dedicated to the mountain gods dotted the path, and one such statue stood winking at passersby with a small pile of coins at its base. I couldn't decide whether his expression wished good luck or was meant to encourage donation. I still had a few pennies in my wallet, so I left them for him, hoping that American currency would bring as much luck as Japanese.

It didn't.

The trees soon parted at the sixth station, *Rokugome*. From here, the land below stretched into the horizon, growing from a canopy of green. Sadly all I saw was gray fog. The trail widened, zigzagging into the mists as the ascent began in earnest. Most people turned back here, satisfied with the forty-minute nature trail.

I climbed into the drifting haze above, and it dampened the sound of other hikers, leaving me isolated with my thoughts. For the first time, I contemplated what I was doing. Here I was, on the other side of the world, and climbing a mountain I'd only seen in pictures or film. The thought invigorated my muscles and drove me on. I'd worked for years to finish my degrees and move out into the world, and now at last I was here.

There's a saying in China, "He who does not reach the Great Wall is not a true man." The Japanese have a similar phrase, *"Fuji-san, ichido mo noboranu baka, nido noboru baka."* This roughly translates as, "He who has never climbed Mt. Fuji is a fool, and he who climbs it twice is a greater fool." In China, I passed my test into manhood, and now I would prove I was no fool.

Still, what about climbing Mt. Fuji twice made you a greater fool?

The path gradually narrowed until the switchbacks stopped at the seventh station, *Nanagome*, a collection of mountain huts offering lodging, overpriced food, and outrageously expensive water. Each hut also offered a special hot iron stamp for your walking stick as proof you'd made it this far. For a price, of course. I leaned on my pole and sighed as the man pressed an iron to my stick.

I felt like such a tourist.

Nanagome, the seventh station. The word *"nana"* in Japanese means "seven," but there's also another word for it, *shichi*. *"Shi"* has connotations with death, so while *Shichigome* means "the seventh station," in liberal interpretation, it could also mean "the death station." Not a particularly pleasant thought and I wondered why my mind focused on that obscure aspect of the Japanese vernacular.

I'd passed hundreds of people on the trail, but it was those in their sixties, seventies, and dare I say eighties that impressed me the most. They huffed, moved slowly, but kept going. Their determination reminded me of Ulrich Inderbinen, a mountain guide who scaled the Matterhorn in the Swiss Alps three-hundred and seventy times, with his last ascent being at the age of ninety. He'd continued to climb other alpine peaks until retiring at ninety-five.

The sky cleared. At last, I could see the top, closer than I'd anticipated. My legs and feet rejoiced. I already felt bruises on the bottom of my feet, and a blister growing under my little toe didn't help. I sat on one of the benches at *Nanagome* and eased my shoes off, spilling out the tiny stones that'd fallen in. My soles were red. It's amazing how much lava rock hurts, even through thick shoes.

Here and there patches of green dotted the brownish slope, and an occasional bird darted about, snatching insects. A small cliff of rock jutted from the top and was the only feature of note. When compared to the Idol and Worshiper on Mt. Teewinot, it wasn't much to look at. Still, that was my goal, and I would meet it before sundown.

The clouds reached and pulled back like wispy fingers grasping for an endless sky. One in particular rose like a menacing shadow over the others, and for the first time, I began to question the wisdom of climbing the tallest mountain in Japan while a tropical storm hovered off the Honshu coast.

Fuji-san's shadow reached over the clouds in a perfect cone. It grew, moving like a stalker through the mists as the hours waned.

The higher I climbed, the more difficult it became to breathe, with each inhale harder than the last. My muscles tingled and my head spun with the beginnings of altitude sickness. Although sleeping in the huts at the top would help me acclimatize, this was going to be a long, headache filled night.

A sinking pit welled in my stomach as I neared the rocky outcropping. There were ten stations, and if I was near the top, why hadn't I come across the eighth yet?

I sighed. Yes, this "top" was the eighth station, *Hachigome*. I looked back at the rocky outcropping I wrongly thought my goal. It now sat at least two or three hundred feet below.

The sky brightened with the last shades of twilight and when the slivers of pinkish sunlight faded, the moon rose like a pale lantern, illuminating distant clouds.

I looked for the altitude marker and my heart sank. I still had more than four hundred and thirty-six meters to go! Fourteen hundred feet! It was like climbing every step in the Empire State Building with another four hundred left to spare.

The man in the last hut looked with trepidation at the path ahead, and advised me to stay there for the night since I hadn't brought a flashlight. I looked up, this time not at a false top, but the real goal. I shook my head. No. I set out to climb this mountain today, and I was going to do it. I came to Japan for the experience, and if I stopped now I might as well turn around and go home. I needed to prove I could do it. If I succeeded, then perhaps I could find a place in the land of the rising sun. I held out my staff and paid the man to stamp it, proof that I'd at least made it this far. He sighed and gave me a knowing look, as if I'd not been the first to ignore his sound advice.

I trudged on, stubborn determination carrying my steps far above *Hachigome*. I looked back at the line of headlamps and flashlights dotting the trail between the seventh and eighth stations. None followed past that point.

I was alone on the mountain, just like I was alone in Japan.

The clouds crept back so slowly that I didn't notice until they'd completely obscured the moon, leaving me in darkness. The rising winds chilled my skin and the last leg of the journey sapped my stamina. At this height, the lack of oxygen makes each step an expression of sheer will. Altitude sickness is a little like having the flu; your skin tingles and all of your muscles lose their strength.

To keep myself going, I counted my steps. One. Two. Three. Every time I reached fifty, I'd stop to catch my breath. Again. One. Two. Three. Ten. Twenty. Or was that Twenty-one? My oxygen-deprived mind lost itself in the simplicities of basic math.

The ninth station, *Kyugome*, was little more than a trail marker. No hot food, no warming huts, and no one to stamp my stick. More rocks had collected inside of my shoes and the throbbing blister on my toe was now the size of my thumbnail. My will to go on faded. I looked back at the "death station" far below and struggled to banish unpleasant thoughts of my own demise.

Then the rain started.

Water pelted my face in gusts that blew me about while I felt my way up the trail with my walking stick. The mountain winds howled, and shivering, I drew my jacket around my neck.

What was I doing? Why was I here? Not just on Mt. Fuji, but in Japan? I stood on the opposite side of the world, with an ocean between me and my home. I wanted independence, freedom, but I was fresh out of college. It was like I'd jumped into the deep end of the pool without checking whether I could swim.

One. Two. Three. The winds whisked my words away. Aching, soaked and chilled, I rounded a bend and squinted to see a torii gate. *Jugome*. The last station! Only two more switchbacks stood between me and a warm blanket. My knees buckled under the pressure, but gasping for breath, I carried myself up and passed through the threshold.

I looked about. Why was it dark?

I walked past the mountain shacks in confused bewilderment. I'd taken too long to get here and they'd closed for the night.

Years earlier, during a particularly cold day in Switzerland I'd gotten caught in *die Bieza*, a bone-chilling winter wind common in the alpine valleys. I experienced a case of mild hypothermia where my core body temperature dropped several degrees. I spend an hour in a warm bath, but it wasn't until about a week later when my body completely recovered.

My frantic knocks on the doors went unheeded, and I brought my knees to my chest as I shivered and slumped against one of the buildings to huddle out of the storm. The air prickled my skin and blew almost as cold as it had in Switzerland, only this time with a chilly rain. I'd conquered the summit of Mt. Fuji, but she wouldn't yield a victory so easily. Was this what it was like actually living out in the world, away from a sheltered college life? I was woefully unprepared for this mountain, so was I likewise unprepared to live away from home?

A group of people from India who'd also braved the hike arrived thirty minutes later, and we kept each other company until someone noticed us and opened the door.

The warm perfume of kerosene rushed into my face as I stepped into the hut. My wet clothes clung to my skin, and after paying the mandatory fee, I took my bed, bunked among dozens of others. The heavy blankets soothed my muscles and I drifted into restless sleep.

I woke to the commotion of hundreds of people. Stumbling from my bunk, tired and stiff, my clothes still wet, I glanced through the crowd. Many had spent the night, but many more had climbed after the rains had died down earlier that morning. Everywhere people slurped small bowls of soba noodles and drank green tea.

I stepped outside and scowled. Clouds had covered the mountain again, obscuring any view of the legendary Fuji sunrise.

I walked the caldera, up above the *Jugome* and away from the crowds. I wanted to be alone when the sun rose, even if I couldn't see it. I stared at the reddening glow, disappointed. All of that effort and no sunrise. Worse yet, the hike back down would probably be nothing but a dull, gray fog.

As if in answer to my disheartened inner voice, or in reward for coming this far, Fuji-san showed compassion, and she parted the vapor.

Below, the clouds rolled in a sea of violet, and above, they coalesced into a ceiling of wavy red. The sky between opened into a narrow corridor that stretched into a horizon of shimmering gold.

Rising like a red orb, the sun peeked over the blanket like a shy child gauging an audience. From the station below, people called to it, raising their hands three times and cheering in unison. "*Banzai! Banzai! Banzai!*"

For five minutes I stared awestruck at the halo of color. For five minutes I was free. Free of care, worry, or pain. My cramped legs became a distant moan, and my headache faded into the first light of the rising sun.

Fuji-san gave me a moment of paradise that I'll ever thank her for. The fog soon rushed across the caldera, again obscuring the horizon and leaving me with a bright, gray haze.

It was enough.

One of the men at the tenth station, *Jugome*, stamped my stick with bright red *kanji*, Japanese characters proving that I'd made it. That stick sits in the corner of my room, and every time I look at it, that red mark serves as a reminder of Fuji-san, and the lessons she taught.

I climb mountains for those rare moments when, in the freedom offered by the high places of the world, I catch a glimpse of beauty and understand what it means to live. Though an ocean stood between me and my home, I now knew I could face what Japan offered. As long as she, from time to time, gave me five minutes.

LITTLE THINGS

E.B. Wheeler

Lieutenant Antonio Rocamora y Sarmiento scanned the noisy, dusty crowd in the marketplace, alert to details. A young nun clutched her rosary and smiled a little too widely at the baker's handsome son. The limping beggar tripped on the cobblestones and caught himself with a strong gait before resuming his shuffle.

The Dominicans of the Inquisition drilled it into the soldiers: watch for the little things. That was the way to catch dissenters, especially the *moriscos* smuggling Arabic texts into the city. Antonio's company had to help find and burn the forbidden papers, along with the people who hid them, if necessary. He shuddered. For a moment, the riot of marketplace smells—fresh bread, fish, sweat, manure—gave way to the remembered stench of blood and waste in the tribunal's jails.

The constant churning of the crowd and the hot sun reflecting off the stone buildings lulled Antonio. He almost overlooked the *morisca* woman.

Her fingers were in constant motion, shifting her basket from one hand to the other, jerking the crucifix away from her neck then patting it back into place. She smoothed her loose, blue cotton Moorish dress to reveal the swelling of her belly.

Antonio's gaze fixed on the woman's stomach. His Maria was just that pregnant, always checking if the baby was moving and placing his hand so he could feel the fluttering kicks, like the gentle flapping of a bird's wings under her tight skin.

Juan, a sergeant in Antonio's company, swooped in on the

morisca. The packed crowd pulled away from them, leaving the woman an island alone in the sea of people. Juan backed her against a stone wall. His rough hands tore away her basket, snatched the veil covering her black hair, groped at the thin fabric protecting her body. She whimpered and huddled against the wall, but the stones were as helpless and unfeeling as the crowd.

Antonio darted through the shoppers and grabbed Juan's hand, jerking him away. The *morisca's* gaze found his for a moment, and he caught his breath. Her wide eyes were the color of amber, framed by long, black lashes. Like Maria's. She probably had a husband at home who'd worry if she was late, as he did when Maria took too long at the market.

"What's going on here?" Antonio asked, dropping Juan's hand like a dirty rag.

"Captain, this woman was acting suspiciously." Juan folded his arms. The *morisca* kept her eyes low. Antonio held out his hand and Juan passed him her veil and basket. He inspected the fragile fabric and passed it back to the woman. Her gaze flicked to his again as she covered her black locks, a questioning gratitude visible for a moment before her expression was as veiled as her hair.

A movement on the ground near her skirt caught Antonio's attention. Something small and white fluttered in the morning breeze. He shifted his foot. "Well, let's see what's in the basket."

He sifted through the loaves of bread and found the thick slab of lamb wrapped in paper.

"Meat! On a Friday!" Juan said, leaning over Antonio's shoulder. He leered. "She's probably smuggling more. Only one way to find out."

He reached for the woman. She shrank against the wall.

Antonio pushed his hand away. "Can't you see she's pregnant, idiot? Exempt from the fast."

Juan stepped back with a scowl. Antonio handed the woman her basket and motioned her away. She fled without a backward glance, off to her waiting husband and their lamb dinner.

"You're such a fool, Juan." Antonio shook his head. "You're supposed to pay attention to details like that."

Juan shrugged and shuffled off. Antonio sighed. He ground the piece of paper trapped beneath his boot, reducing it to illegible white flecks. If Juan had sharper senses, he would've heard the rustle of paper under the woman's dress, but he was blind to things large as well as small.

The guilt Antonio expected never came. After all, what a person believed—the secrets of their heart, their private devotions—these were issues of great consequence. His orders were to focus on the little things.

VOLATILE WHEN MIXED

Tim Tarbet

My dad has a Ph.D. in synthetic organic chemistry, so I've lived around science all my life. Before my dad got his own lab, my mom would complain that her pots and pans were used more for chemistry than for cooking.

Since child labor is cheaper than hiring employees, my siblings and I all worked in his lab when we got old enough. Some of us did better than others. My oldest sister once organized all my dad's chemicals according to the color on their label.

My father was not happy.

I learned a lot of things working in my dad's lab, but I think the most important thing I learned is about spontaneous reactions. A spontaneous reaction is a reaction that will happen when all of the ingredients are present, like when you put a clump of sodium metal in a glass of water. By introducing the two, they immediately conspire to exchange electrons and change their chemical makeup, a true chemical romance.

Of course, spontaneous reactions tend to be some of the most dangerous ones, because once they start you can't just take them off the burner and expect them to stop.

I learned this the hard way.

I was working for my dad one summer doing frac water biocide down in Texas. It was a dull job that involved a lot of driving, getting up at obscene hours, and dumping and mixing chemicals. My coworker,

Daniel, and I were getting ready for the long drive down when my dad, at once the founder, owner, and head chemist of the company, pulled us aside and told us that company policy had changed. Before we had used a cocktail of mild chemicals to create a potent biocide to sterilize the millions of gallons of water that the fracking companies use when they drill their wells, but he'd revised the ingredients that we used, and he said over and over that we couldn't pre-mix the chemicals any more. He was rather insistent on this point, though he never mentioned exactly why, as is typical of my dad. Even today, he tends to assume that everyone else knows as much about chemistry as he does, and always seems a little surprised when we don't. It was already late enough that getting up for the drive would be difficult, so instead of asking questions, Daniel and I reassured him again and again that we would not pre-mix the chemicals.

We set out at six in the morning for Texas, two ten-hour days of driving. We drove and talked and drove and napped and drove some more. We stopped at Subway after Subway to eat, and slept at the hotel with the paintings of Native Americans all over the walls. We drove through the endless red sand and winding canyons of Southern Utah, Nevada, and New Mexico, then finally the sagebrush and rolling green hills of Texas. Early in the evening, we arrived at the company house that the out-of-town workers used, which had little more than a small TV, some fold up lawn-chairs, stools, cold cereal, and four cramped bedrooms.

The next morning we met up with my uncle Ross and our supervisor and spent the rest of the day loading chemicals into trucks, checking equipment, and planning for the coming jobs. Daniel would go to one natural gas well, and Ross and I would go to another. Once all the chemicals and equipment were ready, we made reservations at hotels closer to our job sites, hitched up the trailers, and headed out.

We left for the job site the next morning at four AM. Most crews usually start by six AM, and it usually takes about an hour to drive out to the site, and another hour to set everything up. Any other morning I would be trying to catch a little more shut eye while Ross drove, or at best I would be dimly aware of the directions the GPS was giving me. This particular morning, however, there was a spectacular thunderstorm right on top of us, and I sat up watching it, giggling like an idiot. There was little rain, but lightning fell almost in time with the windshield wipers. The storm stretched to every horizon, and the white hot bolts danced in the darkness like fey ballerinas, there and then gone again, some far, some close enough to make my chest rattle. It was like driving through a fireworks display.

By the time we got to the job site, the lightning had calmed down, but the air was thick with humidity. We were almost swimming as we backed the trailer into position, got the massive hoses all hooked into the right positions, and primed the various generators and pumps we used. I'd done it so many times that muscle memory simply took over.

We'd arrived early enough that the guys in charge of the water hadn't started their pumps yet, which meant we couldn't fill our massive mixing tank, so with else left to do, I decided to get our chemicals ready. I jumped into the truck bed, pulled out an empty bucket, and cracked open the storage containers.

Two big scoops of chemical one, one scoop of chemical two, and a small scoop of chemical three, all into a five gallon bucket.

The reason we'd never worried about pre-mixing the chemicals before was because without the final ingredient, water, the reaction cannot start. As someone from one of the drier states in the nation, it didn't occur to me that air, especially right after a thunderstorm, could be an excellent source of water.

By the time I had finished dumping the last of chemical three in, there was a thin yellow haze rising where the bone white flakes of chemicals met the bucket. A little strange, but nothing to worry about. Our product was a dissolved gas, neon yellow in color. I put the scoops away and put the lids back on the chemicals, ready to jump down and see if the water guys had started the pumps yet.

At this point I realized that I had the trailer with the thousand-gallon tank instead of the one with two five-hundred gallon ones; I needed to make a double batch. I got the chemicals open again and started dumping in more of chemical one. With the first scoop, the smoke turned from a few wisps of yellow to a thick, noxious brown. By the time I dumped in the second scoop, a bright orange flame erupted right from the middle of the mixture, something like a miniature vindictive volcano.

At that moment, a number of things went through my head. The first was that the way I had layered the chemicals ensured that the reaction I had accidentally started would be an explosive one. Second, the truck bed I was standing in had enough chemicals in it to make most car bombers jealous. Lastly, we were standing on top of a natural gas well with a direct pipeline to over a million cubic meters of the stuff.

God himself would not be able to save us.

I grabbed the bucket handle. My accidental volcano was doing its utmost to imitate Vesuvius, spewing pyroclastic flakes all over my hand

and embedding the flaming chemicals in my flesh, but the threat of going home in a snuff box was more than enough for me to keep a grip on the handle. I tossed the bucket off the truck bed, doing my best to dump the contents out as much as possible. I couldn't stop the reaction now, but I could avoid an explosion.

I jumped to the ground, car bomb diffused, but the reaction was proceeding more vigorously than ever, a miniature hellscape on Texan soil. Ross stood nearby, completely dumbfounded. By this point, the fire was hot enough to contend with some bonfires, and I was sure that trying to stomp the flames out would only result in melted boots and flaming trousers, so I yelled for him to go get a fire extinguisher. He was gone before I finished yelling, while I stayed there, hoping that my chemical fire didn't turn into a prairie fire.

At this point, I heard shouting behind me. It was the Mexicans from the water crew running toward me with the most beautiful red cylinder I had ever seen.

God only knows why a water crew would have a fire extinguisher, but at that moment I didn't give a damn.

Salvation.

I ran to them, meeting them halfway, then beat them back to the site of the disaster. Just as I was beginning to drown the violent chemistry in white fog, my uncle returned with every man working on the drilling site, half a dozen of whom had fire extinguishers of their own.

My little disaster quickly gave way beneath the furious onslaught, leaving nothing but a black scab on the ground. Not even the metal handle had survived the inferno.

"Who's in charge here?"

Despite my uncle Ross being twenty years my senior, I meekly raised my voice, "I am."

Considering I had just endangered the lives of a dozen men, more than a million dollars worth of equipment, and far more than that in both environmental and public fallout, I think what came next went rather well.

For the next half an hour I was berated by six feet and two hundred and fifty pounds of angry Texan who raked me over the coals for everything from my youth to my clothes to our lack of established safety procedures in front of all the men there. I don't remember all of the things he yelled at me for, but I do remember most of my answers. "Yes, sir. No, sir. I don't know, sir."

Eventually he ran out of steam, and I was able to worm my way out of any more public humiliation with the excuse, "I need to call my boss."

Once safely inside the truck, I made the call.

"Dad? We've had an incident…"

POISON WITHIN

Marie Tollstrup

"Don't get near my toe, or you'll have a fight on your hands," Dad said, pointing to his right toe.

Dad's ulcerated big toe, gray and swollen, dominated my visit to Sunnyvale Nursing Home. Dad had just turned eighty. Birthday cards from my siblings and me decorated his bedside table. Looking outside Dad's window, Mom said, "Let's take advantage of the sunshine." Anything to distract Dad from his habitual stance to dominate would help.

As I wheeled him out into the garden's sun, Dad muttered to Mom, "Wha' ya see in 'im?" He quoted one of his taunting lines I remembered from my youth.

Astounded, I caught my breath. His words branded my heart. Dad's accusatory tone was alive like it had been in my childhood. Like a slow-growing cancer, his implication of Mom's infidelity metastasized throughout our childhood lives. It swelled within us.

On the long drive home through a beating rain, I relived graphic scenes of over forty years ago. I remembered doors slamming, jarring my sleep. I tried to fall back into my vivid dream. I heard Dad mutter, and then a distinct scream. I wondered if the sharp voices were from my dream down by the river or inside the darkness of my own home. If the walls of my childhood home had tape-recorded my battling parents, it would be a reoccurring horror movie featuring yelling and blood. Mom wailed, and I panicked.

I sat bolt upright in bed, listening intently. Through the second-story bedroom window, the moon, captured in racing clouds, momentarily distracted me. The cacophony of thrashing trees on our front lawn echoed in my room like a discordant song. I heard running, and a door banged shut. What was going on? Was Dad after Mom again?

"Le' me in!" Dad said. His words ate into my heart. He banged on the bathroom door, growling. I prayed the old lock would hold and their scuffle end.

"W'y ja do it?" Dad said in his thick tongue.

"I never did anything," Mom said.

My mind raced, wondering why Dad attacked Mom. Dad said, slurring his words. "Ya saw 'im, din't ya?" Dishes crashed to the floor.

"Don't wake the kids," Mom said. Their fight continued. I heard stifled cries.

"Wha' ya see in 'im? I know ya di' it!" Dad's words pelted me.

"It's all a lie. Your drinks are talking," Mom said. "Weren't you hungry for supper?"

Who were they fighting about now? I heard more grunts and blows and pictured two animals fighting in mortal combat. Pulling the blankets over my head for protection, I attempted to deafen the strident sounds the darkness carried.

I felt alone and powerless. I did not move. My breath was stagnant. I had forgotten I went to bed with a sore throat, but I knew what I witnessed was a living nightmare, a heartache coiling around my soul.

Awakening, I doubted if I ever fell back asleep. I remembered thrashing in bed. My sore throat screamed, and my ears throbbed. I dreaded seeing Mom and Dad that morning for fear I would observe them fighting.

When my sisters and I entered the kitchen, we saw the visible signs of the fight we had heard the night before. Mom's sagging, short sleeved dress did not cover the scratches and bruises on her face and arms. Her eyes avoided ours, and her bent body leaned on the sink. We stared, but Mom said nothing. We were wise enough not to question her.

Dad appeared, filling the kitchen door. It surprised me to see him wearing battle signs because his solid build and added height gave him an advantage over Mom. His marred face and dark eyes met ours. I secretly cheered. Mom had held her own to some degree and got her licks in, too. What a tragic scene, observing two adults at close range, displaying signs of struggle we knew happened under cover of night. How strange that these two adversarial adults were my Mom and Dad.

None of us talked about their nocturnal conflicts. Our own scars lay buried deeply within our souls. Only our staring eyes admitted our vulnerability. We remained bereft like skiffs at sea. The thin walls of the little house on the corner held all our secrets, secrets that became part of its foundation.

Often we heard raised voices. I never witnessed any good coming from my parents' yelling matches and physical confrontations in the depths of night. Weeks would pass, maybe months, but without warning, our sleep would be disrupted. When we moved would the walls of the big house up the hill record new battles?

Dad usually sat down with us at our evening meal, but the nights he did not show, a knot in my stomach twisted and made me uneasy about his absence. Sometimes Dad drank at Al's Tavern in Phlox just to shoot the breeze with fellow farmers up town. But at times he did have the good sense to quit drinking and come home to eat. He loved to joke and laugh with neighbors and strangers, spinning yarns, entertaining anyone who would stand around and listen, especially if the tall tales were about raising potatoes.

Mom finally said, "I don't know where your father is, but let's sit down and eat." I followed her worried eyes as she passed the broccoli, roast, and potatoes. I ate, but every bite sat heavy in my stomach as if I had swallowed lead.

Why Dad acted more polite and engaging with outsiders than with Mom remained a mystery. His combative spirit was stoked the moment he entered the house. Although Dad was addicted to growing potatoes, its demanding gambling risks got to him at times. Al and his buddies became his captive audience all afternoon.

"You didn't hear this one. Happened in '58 when we had an early freeze, remember that?" Dad said between sips of Michelob. "We worked till midnight for two nights straight to harvest two fields of Idaho potatoes." He laughed. "Do you know what we used to see? The full moon's spotlight plus the truck's and car's headlights. But we got 'em in the warehouse." Alcohol released his deep-seated paranoia, unleashing destructive impulses that tore away at all that was sacred. No outsider ever suspected Dad transformed into a brooding accuser when he walked through our door.

Six months later I awoke to snarling growls and slamming doors. Instinctively I pulled my blanket up over my head to protect myself from possible attack and to extinguish the ensuing confrontation. Dad ignored the fact that Mom went to bed exhausted. She had more difficulty getting around now in her second trimester. I heard a piercing scream, followed by gasping groans that cut me like a whip. Blackness smothered me.

It had to be the same perennial argument. Whose child was Mom carrying? Dad's liquor-soaked brain exacerbated his suspicions, and like a scratched record, he accused Mom of infidelity. What an absurd accusation! Mom was never even flirtatious, much less attracted to anyone else in our small town.

After my dad drank, I did not recognize the unsteady, growling man who walked into our home. How could this be my self-possessed, successful father who negotiated loans from the bank so he could buy a new tractor and potato harvester? The man I called my dad would transform into a mumbling paranoid stalker on the prowl, seeking to confront my mother. I prayed this torment would end for my innocent Mom. Her rock-like strength preserved her composure, but for how long? I wondered how many living nightmares my siblings and I would witness.

The light of day ripped away the veil that hid our night terrors. Mom hobbled into the dining room and placed a bowl of steaming oatmeal on the table. A twisted Ace bandage snaked its way around her swollen right ankle. Despite her Spartan face, I saw agony sketched in each step she took. It would be a challenge to carry our next brother or sister plus take care of my four siblings and me.

Last night's stinging scream replayed in my ears. I was an off-scene witness to my Mom's sprained ankle. Somehow Dad's alcoholic paranoia attacked my mother, a pregnant woman. Being on her feet during the day made Mom's right ankle grow to twice the size of her left one. Even I knew she should have gone to the doctor and had it x-rayed.

Thirty years later when she was having her varicose veins removed, a doctor x-rayed her right ankle. What he found amazed him. My mother's ankle had been fractured in three places. It had never been set properly, and now she suffered from its long-term effects, being prone to an aching, swollen ankle.

Mom admitted that what she thought was a severely sprained ankle happened during the night while she carried Johnny. Nothing could be done now to reset her ankle. She had lived too long with those twisted bones. Perhaps the only saving grace that helped her on that tormented night so long ago was that Ace bandage, coiling her ankle. It acted as a crude cast that set her ankle to a degree.

Many years later Mom did have a cast on her right leg. Two days before she died of congestive heart failure, just prior to my last good-bye on Sunday, she begged me to remove it. I, of course, could not comply. She had fallen on a cold January night a month before and sustained a hairline fracture which modern x-rays detected without delay. The sad thing is my mom never walked alone again without support. She died encumbered with a cast, the cast she should have had on her ankle forty-six years prior.

To this day, I try to fathom the degree of anguish my mother endured during this pregnancy. She not only sustained Dad's taunting abuse, but also attempted to walk on a fractured ankle. John, that newborn, became her favorite. Theirs was a bond of survival against all odds. For years John became Mom's champion, distracting Dad and doing his bidding, so Mom could enjoy some tranquility. John's broad Dutch body structure resembled Mom's own Dad's body build, the man who held Mom in his heart. John inherited his grandfather's largesse of heart, their spirits vibrating in tune.

Only years later did bits and pieces of our dysfunctional family's puzzle come to light, so we siblings realized we witnessed domestic violence and what precipitated it. Never once did anyone directly address the healing of our wounds. No one admitted mental illness existed, much less acknowledged that alcohol use exacerbated my father's psychotic condition, leaving incalculable damage in its wake. Even today dealing with mental illness is a delicate on-going issue.

When I was twenty, Mom and Dad were celebrating, better stated, surviving their twenty-fifth wedding anniversary. I received a phone call from Mom at college. Mom said, "Dad's at Marshfield Hospital, getting special help."

"What kind?"

"It's a long story I can tell you now." Weariness clouded Mom's voice. "Your dad thought the IRS was after him. His obsession grew. He thought the house was bugged, and he'd be audited. He wandered around the house mumbling instead of working in the field or warehouse."

"You're kidding. Dad always went to work. He's an award-winning potato farmer at the state level," I said.

"I finally convinced him to see Dr. Mock about his fears."

Mom's voice perked up. "You know, your Dad adores talking to anyone about himself, so he agreed to go."

"What's the bottom line, Mom? What's really wrong with Dad?"

"Shirley, your Dad was diagnosed as a paranoid schizophrenic right after you were born. He was institutionalized and received shock treatments." She hesitated before she went on. "I was overwhelmed, but the slap in my face came when I learned this from my mother-in-law. His folks insisted the doctor only communicate with them."

I detected hurt in Mom's voice. Her words bore through me. We should have been told sooner. Shock treatments. Paranoid. Schizophrenic. I was stunned and bewildered. I felt someone had punched me in the stomach. I sat down to breathe easier, still clinging to the phone.

"Mom, you've lived a tough life. Now I understand the anger and chaos at home, often erupting without reason." I exhaled into the mouthpiece. "The worst fights happened when Dad drank all day. Why would Dad's parents reveal the truth to you?"

"They wanted to explain his extended stay and your dad's unusual behavior. His folks admitted he inherited a brain disease, making it difficult to handle stress." Mom's strong voice impressed me. "You're right. Alcohol seemed to bring on your dad's fighting moods."

"Did Dad have more shock treatments? They sound barbaric." My voice was unsteady. "Do they work?"

"According to Dr. Mock, shock treatments destroy some obsessive memories that plague paranoid patients. Your dad's improved each time he's had shock treatments."

"Mom, you're a marvel." At that moment I wanted to hug her long and hard. "How did you remain sane all these years? You're the one who's been stressed."

"Thanks. I've got to go. Someday we'll chat longer." Weariness crept into her voice.

"Your designed twenty-fifth wedding anniversary card was beautiful. How thoughtful, Shirley."

"Glad you received it on time. I celebrate your endurance all these years. I love you, Mom. Say hello to everyone," I said, feeling spent.

"I love you, too." I heard the dial tone. I froze. How could Mom celebrate a wedding anniversary in the face of unhappiness endured over twenty-five years?

In some real sense, I had escaped, run away from home when I decided to attend college two hundred miles from home. But hearing my Mom's voice brought a pang of nostalgia. I missed the Red River and the wooded back forty. But most of all, I missed my baby sister Linda. I had cared for her like she was my own daughter, changing more diapers than I cared to count.

The hall's horizon stretched in front of me. I walked toward it, wrapped in thought. Mom's marriage was like savoring her favorite meal but contaminated with a deadly poison. Each bite was deceptive. The seemingly delectable exterior hid her demise.

My heels struck the terrazzo, echoing in the hollow emptiness, my mind still in a whirl. How had Mom survived this confusing darkness in her marriage? How had she protected her children to a degree from its sting? Her inner peace was bought at a great price despite the poison within. I whispered, head tilted toward the ceiling, "Will I ever say *I do?*"

Sunnyvale Nursing Home lived up to its name. Dad created his new kingdom there. With his *Wallstreet Journal* at the ready, he gained a new listening audience who he regaled with his tales and led the rosary with his Catholic friends. Because he paid for his care in full, the nurses gave him preferential treatment. Dad was rewarded with the limelight he always craved.

Mom called six months later to update me. "Remember your Dad's ulcerated toe from your last visit? It's gangrened and has to be amputated due to a lack of circulation."

Hearing the verdict, I said, "Dad must be mad. How will he get around?

"He'll miss standing on two feet, but he likes his wheelchair. More and more he's relied on it due to his crippling rheumatoid arthritis."

I took a deep breath. "Mom, could it be karma?"

I heard Mom's deep sigh over the phone. She whispered, "Karma likes to call when we least expect it."

HARD SADDLE ON A COLD DAY

Jeffery Bateman

Ol' Skeets told me that Mustang was dead broke, never bucked him once.
Now I ain't sayin' Skeets lied, 'cause he's a big fella, ya know.
But man! that Mustang sent me flyin' though it's the landin' I object to.

Ain't advice helpful, after the fact?
It's cold out, cowboy, warm up that saddle, warm up his back.
Now I knew it was cold, any fool could see that,
But I figured he'd warm up on the range as we rode,
like the cow pony Skeets said he was.
Now I ain't callin' no one a liar, mind you.
I jus' didn't know I bought me a show pony who needs
a blanky and a round pen to warm up.

So I got on that Mustang that cold December 'morn.
I knew he weren't right soon as I got up on 'em.
He was interested in doing nuthin',
in particular nuthin' I asked him to do.
I squeezed with both legs and told 'em to walk-on,
He started backin' up!
I tried to supple him up some,
He was about as fluid as a three day turd froze in a puddle.
I pulled back on his reins and clucked, so he backed up some.
I'd call that progress, 'cept I already knew he liked to back up.

Well we finally got him walking-on, mostly in a straight line.
I decided to jog him around to sort him out a bit.
His jog is real nice, you could ride it all day. But not that day.
Felt like a pogo stick without the dang spring.

This is where I figured lopin' him was the best idea.
You might feel you should offer your own two cents right about now.

My friend it is far too late for that.

That Mustang did not pick up the trot too smoothly,
and it seemed like he no longer knew the cue for lopin' whatsoever.
The gentle application of a rolling spur struck me as just the thing.

Well, Sir, like most truly great wrecks,
I have no idea what the hell happened next.
I do recall being forward in my saddle,
off balance, tryin' to exert my will.

I opened my eyes and I was layin' on my back,
My riding partner Joe was holdin' my neck.
Off to my left I could see that Mustang just standin' there,
as if he had no earthly idea how I'd got down on the ground so fast.

I'm sure this would puzzle Skeets too, 'cause I ain't calling no one a liar.

Now I knew the wind was knocked outta me, so I didn't panic, much,
even though I couldn't get no air in my lungs.
I took me a mental tour, trying to figure out if I was really hurt,
or jest banged up.

Havin' opted for "jest banged up," I slowly rose,
givin' some thought to my lost dignity,
and the obvious need to get "back in the saddle."

Joe handed me my hat, and as I put in on, I went to smooth my hair,
only to discover a bunch of dirt embedded in my scalp.
Well, that's one mystery solved. Good thing my noggin broke my fall!

Now here comes all them armchair cowboys.
You shoulda hung on to that lariat, boy!
Stuck your feet way forward, pulled his head around.
Yup. Maybe. I'll ask that Mustang to kindly give me a wink

next time he gets the urge to eject me Maxwell Smart style.

But meanwhile, I think I'll just stop listening to Skeets.
That boy's a dang liar.

THE BLUE FEATHER

Julie Walton

Matthew Watkins hitched his riding horse to the wagon. The children and their belongings were already loaded. Holding back tears, his wife Kate kissed each of her three children as they leaned over the wagon's side. Then Matthew embraced and kissed his wife, whispering, "I'll be back. You'll see."

"Please Matthew, don't go. Give up the mail contract! I can't stay here alone; I'm afraid of the Indians." Tears escaped.

"Kate, you must stay—my life might depend on it. The various Ute tribes watch our place, and they know I take the mail regularly from Bluff City to Cortez. If they see me send my wife into town for protection, I will appear weak and afraid," Matt tried to reassure her. "The children will be with your sister in town at the fort. And I'll leave Uncle Tibs with you."

"You must not," Kate sobbed. "That dog has saved you from danger many times."

"Shh. Tibs will stay here and protect you. I will be fine. Do not fear." Dropping his voice, Matt said, "Not in front of the children, Kate." He kissed her again, silencing her protests.

Taking a deep breath, Kate said, "I love you, Mr. Watkins, but you should stay."

Standing at the cabin door, she watched the wagon disappear wiping away tears. Though the sun shone bright, Kate feared the unpredictable spring weather and Indian troubles. *Might as well get some work done,* she thought.

Threatening storm clouds replaced the earlier sunshine. As Kate finished the morning chores, she heard horses coming down the road and grabbed the rifle. Glancing out the window, Kate saw four neighbors on horseback. Relieved, she leaned the rifle against the wall and went to greet them.

"Good afternoon, gentlemen."

"Good day, Mrs. Watkins," said Mr. Williams. "Where's Matthew?"

"Gone to get the mail from Cortez."

"Hmm. We will escort you into Mancos. The Indians are warring, and you ain't safe on your own."

"Yes, I know. But I am staying where I am," Kate said.

"Do not be foolish, Mrs. Watkins. With Matthew away, he'd want us to take you to town." He looked to his companions for support. They nodded in agreement.

"No, he *told* me to stay while he goes away. The children are safe in town. Appreciate your concern, but I must get back to work." Never had she talked like this to a man.

"Those savages prowl around here. You're a woman—a white woman. And they can't be trusted," Mr. Williams argued.

"I am staying." Kate's knees wobbled.

Mr. Williams scowled as he turned his horse to go. "In all due respect, ma'am, I hope we do not have to come back to bury you!" The other men tipped their hats and followed Mr. Williams. Kate watched them leave and thought the weather matched the foul mood. She felt the first raindrops as she went back into the cabin.

Rain turned to snow as the sun went down. The spring storm intensified as the evening progressed. The wind screamed outside but inside was a deafening silence, neither children's voices nor her husband's nightly reading. Kate blew the lamps out, all but one. She placed a kerosene light in the window, a tradition she had begun years ago when Matt began to deliver the mail. Kate changed into her warm nightgown and prayed silently for God to watch over them all. Getting into her cold bed, she immediately missed Matthew's warmth and tried to sleep.

With a jerk, Kate woke to warning growls from Uncle Tibs. She put a blanket around her shoulders. Slipping her bare feet into shoes, she hurried to the door, grabbing the rifle.

"I'm warning you, I have a gun," she shouted through the door.

Peeking out the window, she saw nothing in the swirling snow. Barking, Uncle Tibs came and stood by her. A figure appeared in her limited vision, covered in white. Moving closer, the figure sank to its knees.

"Quiet Tibs," she commanded. *Should I help? What if Matthew was caught in this blizzard needing help?*

With trembling fingers, Kate unlatched the door, holding the gun ready. A shock of bitter cold wind startled her. She saw an Indian; his body stiff with cold as he lay in the snow. *Was he alone? Were there more, waiting to attack?*

Matthew says he 'fears no white man, nor Indian.' Matt would help him.

Kate willed herself to leave the house, got the man back to his feet, and together they stumbled out of the blizzard. She helped him to a chair by the fireplace. It had died down to coals, so Kate put more kindling on. *My light for Matt must have guided him.*

She pried away his frozen blanket, revealing soaked clothing. With his eyes closed, he looked near death. *Caught in the storm.*

Fear was overruled by practicality as Kate worked to save the Indian. She placed water on the cook stove to warm his feet and for coffee, and then added wood to the small blaze to get a roaring fire. With shaky hands, she took off all the man's wet clothes and wrapped her quilts around him. *This was probably not what Matt had in mind.*

Kate removed the man's knee-length moccasins. *No frostbite, but his feet are like ice.* She massaged them, reminded of doing the same for Matt on winter nights. The Indian groaned. *Good sign. He must have some feeling.* She placed his feet in tepid water from the stove.

The Indian's long, thick black hair hung down in two frozen braids, which Kate undid and used her fingers to rake out the melting chunks of ice. Carefully, she removed a beautiful blue feather from the leather tie and placed it on the mantel. She felt his face—still cold.

Pouring a cup of coffee, Kate brought it to the Indian's lips. He did not respond. Not knowing if he knew English, she said, "Please drink. It will help you."

He moved his head; she held the cup while he took a sip, then another. The Indian mumbled a few words that Kate did not understand. Drying his feet, she pulled Matthew's socks on him. The Indian's body started shaking and his teeth chattered.

What more can I do?

There was only one thing she could think of to help him. *It is for his own good, but would Matthew disapprove?*

She took all the bedding and placed quilts from the children's bed on the hearth in front of the fire. Unwrapping the coverings from around the Indian, Kate guided the shivering man to the blankets on the hearth. She covered the remaining blankets over the man.

I cannot do this.

Yes, you can Kate. And you must or he will die.

She forced herself to lay down beside him, covering them both, embracing his naked body with her warmth. She wrinkled her nose at his strong, foreign scent. Trying to distract herself, Kate sang an old lullaby to herself.

"Lullaby, lullaby, nothing to fear; Lullaby, lullaby, angels are near…"

She knew he didn't understand the words but the soothing melody calmed her nerves, and soon his shaking subsided. Exhausted, they both fell asleep.

છ

Uncle Tibs licked her face. *How odd. The dog never gets on my bed.* A dull morning light appeared in the windows. *It must be snowing.* She saw a man, not her husband lying next to her! The events from the previous night flooded in. She still wore her clothes from yesterday. Wanting far away quickly, Kate got up, washed and put on a fresh apron in her room. She remembered the morning chores, and after stirring the dying embers of the early morning fire, she left the sleeping man.

Two-foot snow drifts greeted her, and the snow was flying. Kate had a difficult time getting to the barn. After milking the cow and feeding the other animals, she gathered eggs and chose a chicken for lunch. Kate chopped its head off and made her way through the snow carrying the milk and the chicken's warm body.

She strained the milk while the breakfast mush cooked, and then approached the stranger. His features softened in the relaxation and warmth of sleep. Kate knelt down next to him with the food. She touched his shoulder gently to wake him. His eyes opened with a groggy look; she helped him drink the warm milk. With his dark, black eyes watching her every move, she nervously spoon-fed him cornmeal mush. Neither of them spoke. Uncle Tibs sat nearby watching over the household.

As he finished the food, the Indian turned over on his side. *He may as well rest. I have work, including plucking that chicken.*

છ

With the smell of biscuits baking in the oven, chicken stewing, Kate dipped out some broth to cool then ate her own lunch. After eating, she woke him again, and he sat up on his own. Her patient allowed her to feed him the broth from the bowl, and then gestured for more.

"Would you like potatoes and meat in it?" she asked. She ladled out another bowl of soup with vegetables and chunks of chicken in it. The man took the bowl from her and ate the chunks of food with his fingers and sipped the broth. She offered him coffee and biscuits, which he also ate, saying nothing.

He set the dishes down on the floor by him and lay back down.

ભ

Dark would come fast with the blizzard raging outside. She checked on the sleeping Indian before starting evening chores early.

Kate called to Uncle Tibs. He trotted over. The dog would accompany her—be her eyes and ears in case she lost her bearings in this storm. "Come Tibs," she said and opened the door. Kate could barely see the barn, as she stepped into the even deeper snow. Wind stung her lungs when she breathed; and she caught snatches of the cow lowing.

After all the animals were fed and settled for the night, Kate headed back to the house. Her fingers so numb inside the mittens, she had a difficult time holding the pail of milk. It was dark, and she couldn't see anything—not even the house. She had forgotten to light the lantern in the house before she left. "Tibs, you're going to lead me."

Tibs held his head high for her to hold on to. Kate trudged through three-foot high drifts. Snow flew all around them erasing her sense of direction. She put her faith in the dog to guide her back to the cabin.

At last, Tibs scratched at the door and Kate undid the outside latch. Exhausted, they both slumped to the floor inside. She closed the door, shutting the storm behind her. It was dark, but the fire cast a small amount of light.

After resting, she stood and lit the lamp in the window, noticing the empty spot by the fireplace. Her breath caught in a sense of concern. *He wouldn't have left in this storm?* she wondered. She whirled around looking for him and saw him bundled up in quilts in her rocking chair. Feeling foolish, she blurted aloud, "There for a moment, I thought maybe you had left. Hungry? I'll warm up stew for supper."

The Indian nodded.

As Kate washed dishes, her visitor sat at the table in blankets, whittling a piece of wood. His clothing hung on hooks near the fire, drying.

"Goodnight, now. I am retiring for the evening." The man didn't acknowledge her. She took half of the bedding off the stack on the hearth. Kate undressed in her bedroom, worrying about an Indian in the other room. She put on her thick nightgown and her husband's sleeping gown too, for extra warmth. After making the bed, she got in and tried to sleep. She was cold—tossed and turned, without her usual quilts and Matthew to keep her warm. Her teeth started chattering.

Kate felt a hand on her shoulder. Her guest gestured and held his hand out implying she should take his coverings. She said thank you and spread the blankets over her bed. The extra quilts provided sufficient warmth. Now that she was comfortable, her worry kicked in. *Am I safe here with an Indian in my house? Should I stay alert?*

As if sensing her unease, he sang quietly in his native tongue—strange, yet beautiful. She heard the sounds drift in from the other room. Kate felt a reassurance that she was safe. Her fear melted away.

☙

The next morning, Kate woke to bright light shining through the cabin's small bedroom window. The storm had broken. She had slept well enough and rolled over to feel chilly coldness. No Matthew. She remembered he had gone to fetch the mail.

The man was gone, the hooks empty. Kate savored her solitude a moment longer, eating her breakfast but knew the animals waited.

Milking the cow, she thought about the children and her husband. *Had the Indians attacked the fort? Was it wise to put your life on the line for mail?*

At lunch, she felt grateful for Uncle Tibs's company. She missed her family. Sniffing and barking, Tibs paced. Then Kate heard two soft knocks. Her heart pounded, and her legs felt weak. She cautiously looked out the front window to see three Indian men carrying their rifles, bows and arrows. Their ferocious painted faces frightened her. They didn't speak, waiting expectantly. Behind them, Kate saw another Indian. Relief bolstered her spirits when she saw a blue feather in his hair—her visitor. She saw calm and courage in him and knew she was safe.

Recognition dawned. *They are hungry and cold.* She opened the door hushing Tibs. Taking off their snowshoes, they came in. Her visitor showed no recognition in his face as he joined his companions.

The men sat down at her table. Kate poured them coffee and offered leftover biscuits. Then she took out some provisions to make a meal. Soon she set hot food before the men, and they ate and talked among themselves. Though her insides felt like jelly, Kate served them seconds.

One by one they went to the fire to warm themselves, and then headed into the cold sunshine and deep snow. The last to leave was her visitor, who picked up Matthew's portrait off the mantel.

"My husband, Matthew," she explained. "He has the mail contract and rides between Cortez and Bluff. But I fear for his safety…" She tried to smile but tension of the last few days had taken its toll. A tear ran down her face.

He replaced the picture, took out the small wooden bird figure he had carved last evening. He set it by the picture and left without looking back.

✑

As the weather warmed, the snow melted and the ground became a muddy mess. Two days after the Indian men took shelter at her home, Kate sat milking the cow again. Emotional turmoil filled her; and she hardly ate.

Kate felt the vibrations of horse hooves before she heard them. Even at a distance, she knew the horse ran at full speed. She walked outside; it was Matthew!

Thank God, you're safe. Please God, watch over our children.

Matthew waved and jumped off the horse. "Oh, I missed you! I have so much to tell you!" he exclaimed. Picking her up, he kissed her hard.

"I have something to tell you too," she said.

"An amazing thing happened—I am damn lucky to be alive!" Matthew walked the horse into the barn to remove the saddle and mailbags.

"I got caught in the blizzard and stayed at the Cortez Post Office. When the storm broke, I took a southern route to avoid more snow but ran right into a group of Indians. Three braves followed me and I knew if they caught me, I would be dead. I rode f or hours. Nearly killed my horse."

"But you escaped somehow?" Anxiety filled her.

"As I entered a small glen, I sensed I was being watched. My horse was exhausted, so I got off and looked for a place to hide, knowing Indians could track me. Everything became still. In the distance, I saw two figures, wondering where the third was off to. I watched them follow me and to my surprise three other Indians came from behind and killed them!"

"What about the third one?"

"I didn't know, because I distinctly counted two men being killed. I realized the danger. The third man snuck up on me so quiet, he would have slit my throat, if it was not for my horse's whinny. No time for my gun. I turned around and attacked him. He was strong, and moments later he had a knife at my neck. I thought of you, and how sorry I was for coming on this trip. I should have listened to you."

Matt started the horse's rubdown. "Then my attacker went limp; eyes rolling back in his head. He was dead, but how? I found a knife embedded in his back and saw another Indian, looking at me. He saved my life, and I don't know why. I came straight back here. I needed to see you."

"Did this Indian have a blue feather in his hair?"

"Why yes. I remember, now that you ask," Matthew said, giving Kate a puzzled look.

Kate knew the answer. This Indian had given her a great gift. Kate looked in her husband's eyes and smiled.

"Maybe you would like to hear about my adventure? Four Indian men came to lunch two days ago. I was frightened but remembered what you said. So I invited them into our cabin and fed them…"

❧

This story is based on my great-great Grandmother Mary Knowlton Coray Roberts born in 1848. She fed Indians during the Ute uprising in 1883 or 84 in Colorado, which led to saving her husband's life. "Two Indians came out of the brush and rode along beside him, one on each side. They told him that he had a brave squaw, as she stayed home and fed the Indians while everyone else went behind the high fence. After a long way, they told Clark that he was safe now and left him. He knew that they had saved his life from the other Indians who were ambushed along the way waiting for him." It comes from *Roberts Family: Connecticut to California*; revised, edited by Irene C. Wayland, 2006, p. 64.

RITUAL

Marie Tollstrup

Traversing the terrain of his scalp,
I hold intimate knowledge
even blind-folded
of each barnacle, mountain, and valley.

Mid-afternoon he leans
over the kitchen sink
for his cleansing ritual.
Slippery soap sifts through fingers.

My hands explore a craggy squamous scab,
a scarlet blossoming basal cell,
an indented silver-dollared skin graft
that transformed a B-B pellet melanoma.

Towels draping his shoulders,
we change venue to the bathroom stool.
Applying Aldara sheen, we pray to war gods
to slay cached cancerous cells.

Alternately we paint cinnamon
Blood Root, Indian war paint,
an antioxidant that eats moles,
warts, and malignant flesh.
We've declared war
emblazoned in orange-rust paste,
battling dashed spirits
and cyclic chameleon growths.

Will we march in victory?

If hands can mold healing,
if love-rituals are the standard,
then triumph we will.

LIVING PICTURES

Sherrie Lynn Clarke

Dressing a dead infant is just like dressing a doll.

Donaven was supposed to wear the outfit my aunt had made for him to church. Instead, he wore it to the graveyard. I hadn't realized how close he was to fitting in it as I slid his cold limbs into the one-piece suit. I suppose I shouldn't have been surprised. Babies grow fast.

The funeral director stood across the table from me, helping me turn Donaven over so I could close the buttons on the back. The clothes fit him perfectly. It looked like he was wearing a two-piece suit: a red plaid vest with a short-sleeve white shirt underneath, dark blue pants, and a bowtie made out of light blue ribbon safety-pinned on to finish off the look. If I hadn't known better, if his skin didn't radiate coldness, if his face didn't look like someone had scrunched or stretched it, I might have assumed he was taking a Sunday afternoon nap.

The funeral director thanked me. He told me someone from some nonprofit organization would be by that day to take pictures and I'd get them on a CD later. He offered his condolences and sent me on my way, the extra ribbon bowtie clenched in my hand.

My aunt made outfits for all her great nieces and nephews. The two-piece suit was made with the same pattern—though modified slightly—as the light blue blessing outfit Donaven wore only two weeks before. My aunt made it for my first son when he was born, and we reused it for Donaven's blessing. It was the same outfit he wore when the last pictures were taken of him alive.

ᴄᴈ

We gathered in the front room to take family pictures after Donaven's blessing. Justin sat on the loveseat, Donaven propped up on his lap. I positioned the camera on the entertainment center, picked up Xen, and sat on the couch next to Justin. Xen wiggled, wanting to get back to what he had been playing with. The self-timer light sped up slowly. Donaven whined quietly. Xen squirmed; I bounced my knee a few times.

"Look at the camera and say cheese," I said through my grinning teeth.

Xen fussed and fidgeted. The camera flashed.

"Let's take a picture of just Donaven," I said before Justin could take the blessing outfit off of Donaven. Xen slid off my lap.

Justin sat on the floor with Donaven and held him up for the picture. Donaven's arms hung awkwardly to the side like a scarecrow. I snapped the shutter. Checking the digital copy, I okayed it and Justin laid Donaven down and started changing his clothes.

I flipped to the image with all of us and grimaced. Xen looked at the camera, but the picture preserved the beginning of a scream. Donaven looked up to the side as if he saw something interesting on the ceiling. So much for a family photo. I went back to the picture of just Donaven. He gazed right at the shutter, his head taking up most of the frame. His eyes seemed to convey some unknown newborn intelligence that I would never understand.

☙

The house was quiet. The thin CD case from the nonprofit organization rested in my hand. With one fluid movement, I opened the case, popped the CD out, snapped the case shut, and slid the disk into my computer. Instead of opening a file with the pictures on it, a video began. The first picture was the same one printed out for the case cover. Donaven in black and white, one ear poking out strangely instead of cuddling against his head, his lipsticked mouth pinched shut as if he were displeased. He'd always slept with his mouth slightly open.

My eyes unfocused as the video scanned through the pictures. My hearing dampened, barely hearing the song meant to bring comfort or tears. Neither came.

Close-ups revealed jarring wrinkles on his fingertips and toes as if his skin were waterlogged. His eyes were glued shut, hard, cold, frozen. A teddy bear I didn't recognize was shoved between his body and arm to make it look like his arm rested on the bear's legs instead of stiffly stuck hovering a few inches above the table. His feet angled awkwardly away from each other, heels touching. He looked like a doll. Or an old man who finally found his rest. I couldn't tell which. Despite the photographer's and the mortuary's efforts, a corpse was still a corpse. Everything about him said stranger. That was not the baby I had nursed.

I never printed them out. The only pictures we printed have a piece of his soul. His eyes are alive. They look at me as if to say, "I'm sorry I couldn't have stayed longer, Mom."

SPAT ON EDEN

C.F. Helms

As a daydream child, I dashed through the door of my aunt's house,
blazing down linoleum-covered stairs into a basement world
that smelled of musty concrete, earth, and newly washed bed sheets.

Once a year, the sickly stench of pickles rose violent and relentless
from a subterranean assembly line, where my aunt stood cramming
cucumbers into jars better used for rescuing bees from the flower bed.

At night, I laid awake trying to ignore the stern, forbidding stare of my
great-grandmother's daguerreotype portrait, disapproval seething
from her black-and-white visage: the essence of Mormon repression.

Story was she took a pitchfork, chased her son clean off her land
for smoking or some obscene word that flew out of his mouth.
Two angels armed with flaming swords enforced his deportation.

In my best friend's basement, thirteen years of age, the angels
stripped me, held me down, their God expelled me from Eden
while His servant probed my innocence and tore it from my grasp.

As a dreamless man I visited the basement world in which I spent
my childhood. The smell of soiled bed sheets and paralyzing terror
filled the room. I spat upon the portrait, spat on Eden, spat on God.

HEALTHY HEART

Lorraine Jeffery

"You're lucky," the doctor said with a smile. "Your heart looks great, and considering your family history, that's saying something. With a father who died of a heart attack at 31, and a mother who's had a bad heart for years, you have a very healthy heart."

"Great!" Kathy said with a smile. "And I appreciate your taking care of my mother all these years. She'll be living with me now, and I'll keep an eye on her."

"That'll be nice," the doctor said, looking at his chart in a distracted manner. It was clear that her examination was over.

There was a spring in Kathy's step as she walked out into the crisp Colorado air. She was looking forward to having her mother living in the apartment at the back of her home. Her daughters were delighted that Grandma was going to be living with them. Her only reservation had been the possible impact it might have on her husband. Craig had quickly agreed to the proposal but Kathy wasn't sure how he would deal with the reality of living with his mother-in-law so close. She hoped Rena would not offer too much advice on how things should be done.

Her mother's health had rapidly declined as the complications with her heart disease became apparent, and although she had been willing to go to an extended care unit, Kathy had persuaded her to come and live in the apartment they had built onto the back of their home. And, as Kathy had known she would, in the end Rena had agreed.

Kathy drove back to her mother's empty house and parked in front of the brick rambler that had been her home before her marriage some fourteen years ago. Now it had fallen to her to clean out the stacks of boxes in the basement so they could sell the house, since her mother would no longer need it.

The basement had the musty odor she remembered from childhood. She glanced at the empty wastebasket that stood next to the stack of boxes she had emptied. Stacked near the door were three boxes which she had refilled with memorabilia from her mother's past. They were waiting for Rena to go through them.

Shortly after she had married, Kathy began encouraging her mother to go through the boxes in the basement, but Rena had brushed her off with excuses about being too busy with her teaching assignments and life in general. Over the years, on and off, Kathy had mentioned the boxes, but nothing had happened.

When her petite mother with the blue-veined hands had agreed to move in with her, Kathy requested that she first go through the boxes in the basement.

"I don't know what you want to keep and what you want to get rid of," she had said. "You're the only one who can decide that."

Rena looked at her and sighed. "I should have gone through them when I had the energy, but I really can't do it now."

Kathy shrugged. "Well, what should we do with them?"

Rena leaned back on the couch and closed her eyes. "You know, I've lived without
whatever is in those boxes all these years. I guess I can continue to live without it." She wrinkled her nose. "You know, I don't even remember what's in most of them. Stuff from your school days, I suppose."

So in the end, Kathy agreed to do the first sorting. She would toss any of her school memorabilia that she didn't want and anything she was pretty sure Rena didn't want. The rest of it, she would repack for her mother to sort through later, a little at a time.

And Kathy was ruthless. She was not by nature a sentimental person and couldn't believe all the report cards and scrawled elementary school pictures that Rena had kept, to say nothing of the various high school awards.

Kathy was an only child and her mother was devoted to her. Her mother's love had warmed her and provided a firm foundation.

It was late afternoon and the light was fading when she pulled one of the final boxes from against the wall. There were only two others left. By now she was sorting through mementos of her mother's life in Paxton, Florida–the years when her father had been alive. He had died when Kathy was only seven and she had few memories of the handsome man with black hair who had worked on the oil rigs off the Florida coast.

She pulled out some fabric and recognized the brown chickens and yellow eggs that had adorned their 1978 kitchen window in Paxton. She reached for a yellowed sheet of paper and saw that it was a "Best Teacher of the Year" award her mother had won in 1977. She smiled, remembering her mother had always been an outstanding teacher, and kids wherever she went had loved high school algebra and geometry. That was a feat in itself.

The next paper Kathy reached for had a blue hue and she saw that it was a death certificate. It had been issued from DeFuniak Springs, the County Seat of Walton, Florida, for Jack Hansen Hartmen, age 31. Her eyes quickly scanned it and she started to add it to the boxes destined for her mother's review, and then she stopped.

"Undetermined," read the line across from "Cause of Death."

"Undetermined?" she said aloud to the empty room and read it again. Her father had died of a heart attack. That's what her mother had told her. *What did 'undetermined' mean?* She wondered.

She remembered that Walton was a small county, even now, and wondered what kind of equipment the coroner had in 1978. *But surely he could have confirmed a heart attack even then,* she thought.

She set the death certificate aside and thought about it as she continued to sort through the box. She looked at the last two boxes but decided she could finish them tomorrow when the light was better and stood up, leaning backward to get the catch out of her back.

Then she picked up the death certificate and went up the stairs to wash her dirty hands before going home to fix dinner.

After homework was done and the girls were playing their computer games, Kathy retrieved the death certificate and went into the apartment to find her mother. Rena was lining the drawers of her dresser and turned when she heard footsteps.

"Don't stop," Kathy said. "I just had a question. Why did you tell me Dad died of a heart attack?" The death certificate says his death was from an undetermined cause."

Her mother kept her back to Kathy until she finished smoothing the liner, and then she turned and sat down on the bed, slowing her labored breathing.

"You were little and needed closure," she said finally. "What would it have accomplished if I'd told you they didn't know why he died? That would just have upset you and you would have kept thinking about it. It was just easier to say 'heart attack' because that's something you had heard about and understood."

"But you should have told me later," Kathy said.

Her mother shrugged. "Didn't think about it later. Besides what does it matter?"

"Yeah, I guess you're right," Kathy said handing her mother the paper. "I was just surprised."

Rena nodded and put the paper in the bottom of the drawer.

"What were his symptoms?" Kathy asked.

Rena closed her paper-thin eyelids and sighed. "It was so long ago. I think he got sick, vomited, ran a fever–that sort of thing. It was an emotional time and I don't remember everything."

Kathy nodded. "He's buried in Paxton, right?"

"Yes," Rena said. She stood up and started stacking folded sweaters into her drawer.

Kathy also stood. "I'm just about finished with the boxes," she said. "Sorry, but I didn't keep all my elementary pictures and stuff from grade school."

"It's up to you," Rena conceded. "I didn't know what you'd want to keep and what you wouldn't so I probably kept a lot of junk I didn't need to."

Later that evening as Kathy packed the dishes in the dishwasher, she thought about her mother's comment. Yes, as a child, she would have worried about her father's death, maybe even wondered if she had somehow been responsible, but her mother's easy lie disquieted her.

It was nine o'clock when she thought about her mother's youngest sister in Santa Monica. *Aunt Barbara will still be awake,* she thought. *It's only eight o'clock there.* Kathy walked into her office, closed the door and looked up her aunt's number.

"How's the beach?" she asked when Barbara answered.

"Heavenly, like always," was the reply. "I still don't know why you and your mother like the mountains more than the beach."

"Well, to tell the truth, I like both," Kathy said. "But I guess Mom got her fill on the Florida Coast."

"Yeah, I guess so," Barbara replied. "How are things going?"

"Good. Mom seems to be making the move all right."

"I'm glad," Barbara said. "I think she'll be happier with you than in a care center."

"I hope so. Hey, Aunt Barbara, I'm calling with kind of a strange question. What do you remember about my father?"

"Not much," Barbara said. Kathy thought she heard a guarded quality in the answer.

"Well, Mom always told me he died of a heart attack, but I was cleaning out boxes today and ran across his death certificate and it says the cause of death was undetermined. Did you know that?"

"Yeah, I did," Barbara said. "I didn't know Rena told you differently. Why would she do that?"

"Well, basically she said it was because I was only seven and would have obsessed about what had killed him if I had known it was undetermined. She said I could understand what a heart attack was."
"Makes sense."

"Yeah it does, but it surprised me," Kathy said.

"I can understand that," her aunt said. "But your mother always said truth was overrated. If it would hurt someone and didn't serve any good purpose, she didn't think it needed to be told. In this case, she probably didn't think it would make any difference."

"Well, my doctor won't be so impressed with my healthy heart," Kathy said and could hear her aunt's laughter on the other end of the line.

She laughed too and then asked, "What was he like? My dad."

Barbara quit laughing and took a breath. "Truth?"

"Truth."

"Well, he wasn't all that great as a person. I never could figure out why Rena picked him. I thought he was controlling and abrasive and I don't think their marriage was all that good. He moved her to Florida, away from her family, so we never knew all the details but I don't think he was all that good to her."

"I wondered," Kathy said. "She never talked much about him and didn't keep many pictures."

"I don't think it was a good time in her life," Barbara said. "And I think the only thing he left her, besides you of course, was his life insurance policy. Interestingly enough, those oil workers had good coverage and that made it a lot easier for her to raise you on a teacher's salary."

"I'm sure that's true," Kathy said. "But then again, she's never said much about that either, other than it was there."

"Well, I'm pretty sure it helped pay for your wedding, among other things."

"I didn't know that," Kathy said. "Well, Craig's working late, so I'd better read a story to Cerise. Mandy's too old for stories, but it's past both of their bedtimes."

"Yeah, it is later there," said Barbara. "Tell your mother 'Hi' for me and call me again sometime. I always enjoy hearing from you."

Kathy thanked her aunt for her information and hung up the phone. Long after the stories, she lay in bed listening to Craig's regular breathing and let her thoughts return to her mother. *How much did truth matter?* She wondered.

She got her children off to school the next day and went back to her mother's house to finish her sorting task. She emptied the wastebasket with yesterday's refuse into the garbage can in the garage and resumed her duties, knowing that once she was done she would have to recruit Craig to haul the repacked boxes out of the basement and over to their house.

The box she started on had several typed algebra lesson plans which were held together with rusty paperclips. She didn't think her mother would want them but she had a hard time tossing out papers that had obviously taken a lot of time and effort. In the end, she put them into one of the "keep" boxes by the door.

She pulled out the final box from the corner. It sagged a bit from the weight of the other boxes that had been stacked on top of it, and the contents felt compacted when she opened it. Again, she sorted quickly through old utility bills and tax returns. Why had her mother kept them? There were a few letters in her mother's loopy handwriting to her Aunt Barbara and her Uncle Keith. She tossed them into a keep box, and picked up another paper in her mother's handwriting. She quickly scanned it and tossed it into the wastebasket. Then she paused, remembering a random conversation she had had with her daughter, Mandy. She reached back down into the box and picked up the paper searching for the words that had caught her attention, "castor beans."

It was a recipe of some kind with no title. The pencil lead had smudged and she could barely make out, "Cook castor beans until soft, strain, mix with solvent." That's all there was, but she remembered Mandy's announcement in the warm kitchen after school had started in September.

"They make ricin poison from castor beans. Did you know that, Mom?"

Kathy had not known that, but she had told Mandy that she knew what a castor bean plant looked like. "We had one behind our garage when I was a kid in Florida," she had said. "I remember it because Mom made such a big deal about me staying away from it. I guess she knew how poisonous it was and I wasn't even allowed to touch it. She picked the beans off the plant herself so no kid would eat one by mistake." Mandy had been interested in her story of childhood.

Kathy put the paper to one side and sat still. Finally, she took a breath and sorted through the rest of the box, filling the wastebasket with bills, receipts and crayoned pictures. She took out the trash, put the yellowed paper in her purse and went home.

Later that evening she looked up ricin on her computer, read the symptoms of ricin poisoning and looked at an image of the plant. Yes, she remembered it.

Then she googled "Jack Hansen Hartman" and kept poking buttons. She finally ended up on a genealogy site that confirmed that the Jack Hansen Hartman on the screen was the one she was looking for. He had been born in Red Bay, Florida to Clifford and Melva Hartman. Rena had told Kathy that her father was an only child and his parents were dead. But she hadn't volunteered any names or shown any interest in contacting other relatives.

Kathy hadn't been interested either, but she was now. She poked a few more buttons and the screen noted a niece named Cindy Hartman. Kathy stopped typing and looked at the name–ra niece might still be alive, but how could she find her? The site offered nothing more, so Kathy wrote the name down and logged off.

She stared at the wall behind her computer. *Do I have family out there somewhere? Do I want to know them? What would Mom think if I tried to contact them after all these years?*

Later, as she prepared for bed, she told Craig that she had googled her father's name and about the niece she had found.

"I always wondered why you've never been curious about that side of the family," he said pulling back the covers.

"Would you have been curious?" she asked.

"Sure. I'm not sure I would have wanted to have a big family reunion with a bunch of cousins I didn't know, but I would have been curious about them. Half of your DNA comes from your dad."

"Yeah," she said slowly. "I'm usually a curious person, but I think I was cautious because of Mom. She never showed any interest, and I wasn't sure how she would take it if I did."

"And now?"

"Now I'm older and have kids of my own and I think I want to know."

Craig nodded and said, "Go for it."

By the next morning, Kathy had a plan. Given, it was a poor plan but it was all she had. She looked up the population of Red Bay, Florida and found it to be less than 4,000. If the Hartman's had lived in that town for any length of time, she reasoned, surely someone would know Cindy Hartman. Kathy started with the four Hartmans in the phone book. She told them she was Jack Hartman's daughter and was looking for her cousin. In less than thirty minutes she had Cindy's number and the phone was picked up on the fifth ring.

"Hello, is this Cindy Hartman?" Kathy asked.

There was a very guarded, "Yes."

"First off," Kathy said. "I'm not selling anything and I'm sorry to bother you, but I was wondering if you were related to Jack Hartman."

There was an audible sigh before Cindy answered. "Yeah, he's my uncle, but he's dead. He died a long time ago. Why do you want to know?"

Kathy took a breath and jumped in. "I'm his daughter. I was born in Paxton and my mom is Rena. Do you know about us?"

"I knew Uncle Jack was married but I didn't know he had a daughter."

"I live in Colorado now," Kathy continued. "I'm married and have two daughters. I haven't had any contact with my dad's family, but now that I have kids of my own, well, I realize that there are contributions from both sides of the family. And I wanted to know something about Dad's family."

"I can't tell you very much," Cindy said. "I'm just his niece. I mean his sister or his mother could tell you a lot more."

Kathy swallowed. *So there had been more lies.* "His mother is alive?"

"Yeah, Aunt Melva lives in Atlanta, but Uncle Cliff died about ten years ago."

"Does she know Jack had a daughter?"

"Gosh, I don't know," Cindy said. "My family doesn't talk to her much and Jack was kind of a black sheep so I can't answer that question. But I think I have her number. Do you want it?"

Kathy paused and thought. *My grandmother's number—do I want it?* She didn't know but finally decided that it wouldn't hurt to have it.

68

She didn't have to call. "Yes, that would be nice," she said.

She repeated the number back, and then asked. "Does his sister live in Atlanta?"

"No, she lives somewhere in Texas but I don't have her number."

"Thanks anyway," Kathy said. "You've been a great help."

Kathy sat in her office for almost twenty minutes before coming out to finish the breakfast dishes. She thought she ought to talk to Craig before confronting her mother, but knew she could not wait until he got home from work, so she walked back to the apartment and knocked on the door.

She heard shuffling footsteps, and then saw her mother's pale face light up with a smile.

"Come in," Rena said. "You don't have to knock."

Kathy sat down on the couch, squared her shoulders and plunged in."I'd like to talk to you about Dad."

Her mother nodded slowly, walked over and turned off the TV. "Okay," she said and settled back into her favorite chair. It was upholstered in bright yellow daisies.

"I've asked you before," Kathy said. "But now I'm an adult and I see things differently. What was Dad like?"

"Charming, Fast-talking. Good-looking," her mother said. "As I told you, he didn't go to college but he was smart and he was a hard worker."

"And his family?"

"He was an only child and his parents were dead."

Kathy pursed her lips. "Actually they weren't. His mother is still alive and lives in Atlanta."

Kathy heard a quick intake of breath.

"Really?" Rena said. "He told me they were dead and they didn't come to the funeral. How do you know his mother's alive?"

"The Internet's a great thing."

Rena looked at the floor and nodded. "Have you talked to her?" she asked softly.

"No," Kathy said. "But I'm thinking about it."

Rena nodded again but didn't say anything.

"So what was your marriage like?" Kathy asked abruptly.

"Her mother shifted in the chair. "Not good. We were happy the first couple of years, but after that. . ." She shook her head. "There were some rough years."

"So you were happier being alone and teaching school?"

Rena looked at her sharply. "In some ways it was easier, but raising a child alone is never easy."

"True. But the insurance money helped."

Her mother stared at her. "There's more to life than money. You know that. I spent a lot of time with you and I've always supported you in everything. I did my best at parenting."

Kathy nodded and smiled. "Yes, you did. And you were, *are* a *great* mom."

Rena smiled and visibly relaxed, slumping a bit in the chair.

"One more thing," Kathy said. "What do you know about ricin poisoning?"

Her mother's jaw tightened and the cords on her neck went taut as she stared at her daughter. Kathy's eyes traveled to her mother's clenched and trembling hands and she knew. It didn't matter what her mother said—she knew.

"What are you asking?" Rena hissed.

"Nothing much," Kathy answered looking back at her steadily. "I just wondered about the truth."

"The truth!" Rena spat. "After twenty-seven years what does it matter?"

"You're right," Kathy said looking at her mother. "You remembered. It was exactly twenty-seven years ago."

Rena clamped her mouth shut and Kathy regarded this small, frail woman with the failing heart who would be living in her home–this woman she didn't know, who may or may not have committed a crime over twenty years ago. But she didn't feel anger. What she felt was an overwhelming rush of sadness as she looked at the small clenched hands.

"It matters," Kathy said finally. "Not because he was my father, but because you're my mother."

She watched as silent tears dropped onto daisies.

MOM'S HOMESTEAD LILACS

Marilyn Ball

Spring is never the same without her lilacs.
How I loved their lavender glow, pressing
my nose in the scented clusters. Years passed,
now in dreams that fragrance wakes me,
and my eyes hauntingly see our backyard gate.
I hear its thudded slam, and there to my left
a cluster of three large -leafed bushes older than me,
greening in spring sun. Touched by some ancient signal,
they burst into bloom, lilac perfume drifts into my heart.
I used to watch first blossoms lure two other bushes
into flower while I swung in the rope swing during
first warm days. Mother's practiced coaxing and work
energized these plants she faithfully tended.

Something about lilacs makes them worthy of a bride's
bouquet, or at the very least, a centerpiece for Sunday dinner.

MUNDANE CHORES

Jodi Milner

The laundry basket skitters away and giggles in the corner of the room. Running away isn't the fun part, it's getting caught. I creep over, tippy toe, tippy toe, and nudge at its corner. It shrieks and scampers across the carpet, an awkward plastic tortoise on steroids.

It's a fun game, at least for a while, at least for him. For me, the dryer needs emptying, the clothes need folding, the boy needs washing, the kitchen needs, well ... everything.

I lift the basket. My son Danny clings spider-like to the underside and peers at me in hope that this is the start of a new game. His eyes shine with a wild curiosity that reminds me of a playful kitten.

"Sorry Buddy, Momma's got work to do, time to get out." I give the basket a gentle shake, and he clings harder.

"No!" he shouts with the same tone normally reserved for hands-on-hips arguments. I imagine him trying to pull the pose now and tumbling out of the basket. The thought makes me smile.

"Suit yourself," I say under my breath and scoop up the basket, boy and all, and lug them to the laundry. Soon warm piles of fresh fragrant laundry are covering us both and I pile shirts, shorts, and socks into the basket. Danny is pretending he's not there and squishes his eyes tight. It won't last, it never does. I toss the final handful on the top of the already unsteady pile and bump the dryer door shut with a metallic bang.

"Mommy? Moooommy?" he calls, his voice muffled beneath the layers of clothes. "Want out now."

"Of course you do." I fight to suppress a sigh and it stuffs itself into a tight knot in the center of my chest. "Hang on, just a sec." I haul the overflowing basket back to the bedroom and spill clothes and boy on the end of the bed. His hair stands out in a halo from the static.

He romps through the clothes, pouncing and rolling in the pile of warm before flopping on his back breathless. "Again, Mommy. Do it again!"

"Uh uh, no way sir. Folding first, then we can play more."

His lip juts, his forehead creases, he slides from the bed and lunges at my leg, pressing his head into my thigh.

"Ah, come on baby. Let's not do this." I fold three more shirts, creasing the sleeves sharply, and think wistfully of my old day job. It used to be that a morning of hard work brought with it a sense of accomplishment, or at least a decent lunch with the other secretaries. These days, a morning of mundane and frustrating work means a lunch of leftovers and funny shaped crackers.

"Mommy, mommy, mommy, mommy…" Danny's protests have disintegrated into a primal chant, a monotonous mantra he will repeat until he gets his way. He leans into my leg to punctuate each syllable. I admire his persistence -for about a minute- before the urge to scream starts kicking in. It's as deeply ingrained as his need for attention, and grows with every passing moment.

"No, no, no, no." I chant back, matching the rhythm to each tuck and fold of a pair of shorts and another shirt. Telling him "no" is useless, it makes him more upset and he begins to yell to drown me out. I'm reminded of the quote, "You can't argue with crazy." Crazy people fight using their own shifting set of bizarre rules. To use logic with them is pointless. Logic is most certainly beyond a two-year-old's grasp. Does that make him crazy? Yes, and yes again.

And yet, I end up arguing with him many times a day about the necessity of wearing clothes, the importance of eating at meal times, the fact that his car seat is not going to eat him, and the requirement of bedtime. If anyone is crazy around here it's probably me.

I fold the last pair of shorts and place it into the basket. Danny's chants grow quieter now and I reach down to pat his head, ruffling his downy hair. He looks up at me while reaching his arms way up high. I pull him close. He pulls me closer until we are squishing our noses together. He giggles. His tiny blue jewel eyes sparkle once again and teach me worlds about what it means to forgive, and forget.

"Mommy," he says with reverence. His voice is full of wonder as if he is trying to fit a whole world of meaning into it.

I kiss the feathery crown of his head and cradle him in my arms. "Baby," I answer, trying to fit all of my heart into that one word.

I pray one day I can live up to everything he sees in me.

A LITTLE MAGIC

Carol Nicolas

"There is no buried treasure!" I glared at my neighbor. The last thing I needed was Letty Smith snooping through my house or yard. I had enough troubles.

"Oh, but you're wrong." Looking like a large, overripe tomato in her best polyester red suit, Letty clutched a rhinestone-studded purse in one hand and an empty measuring cup in the other as she craned her neck and tried to peer around me. I kept the half-opened door anchored with my foot.

Of course I was familiar with the tale of the fabulous emerald and diamond necklace, stolen from a noblewoman who had been visiting Boston from England in the late 1700's. The thief had supposedly buried the necklace somewhere on his farm outside Boston. When he refused to divulge its location, he was hanged and the information lost. His poor wife and child had been left to struggle on alone. That child had grown up to be my fifth great-grandfather, Robert McNally. At first, the McNally's had refused to sell the land to anyone in hopes that the necklace would turn up. The reward alone would have paid off their mortgage and kept them comfortable for life. But as the years turned into centuries, and the family's financial difficulties continued, the land had been sold off bit by bit until only this house and its surrounding acre of lawn and trees remained. Yes, I knew the story. I just didn't believe it.

I sighed and turned my attention back to Letty. "Mrs. Smith, I assure you, the entire property has been gone over with metal detectors, shovels, and even divining rods. There is no treasure. There probably never was. It's just one of those stories that get passed down through the years."

Letty Smith pursed her fleshy, brilliant red lips and stared down her nose at me. Her muddy eyes reflected her disbelief in my words. "Why then did your grandmother put up a tall fence and guard the property with a pit bull? Why did she shoot off a twenty-two whenever a salesman came to the door?"

I grimaced. "Maybe she just didn't like salesmen."

Granny McNally used to tell me stories about how people were forever trespassing on their property, looking for the buried treasure. Early in her marriage, she had got up one night to find some men digging up her thriving vegetable garden. She was so angry that she bought a pit bull and a rifle, and she used them in that order. (Grandpa was amused. He had never liked salesmen or trespassers either.) Granny earned a reputation for being a tough old bird, but she was fond of me.

I was the last of four daughters, with no marriage prospects and only a high school degree. While my sisters danced and partied their way through high school and college (in spite of which, still managing to obtain high grades, good jobs, and marriages), I visited Granny and listened to her stories. When I complained about my lack of beauty and ardent admirers, Granny fondly patted my hand and said, "Never mind, dear. You're a late bloomer, that's all. You've got talents your sisters don't have. Focus on developing them, and love will come to you eventually."

Two years ago, Granny died. No one was more surprised than I was when the will was read, and I was named her heir. In spite of protests from my parents and sisters, I inherited this house and its contents, along with Granny's antique shop in Boston. What followed was an intensive period of learning while I struggled to make sense of her bookkeeping, find lost items for irate customers, and keep the taxes paid. I also moved into her house, thus inheriting the headache of the legend of the lost necklace.

Letty cleared her throat, interrupting my thoughts. "Your grandmother refused to let anyone conduct a search. She terrorized the neighbors along the street. She even pointed that rifle at me, and all I wanted was to bring over some freshly-baked chocolate chip cookies." Letty pouted.

I sighed. When I had first moved in, Letty had been on my doorstep with her cookies and complaints. "I do hope you will be a better neighbor than your grandmother was," she said.

"Probably not," I thought to myself. In the past two years, Letty had tried all kinds of schemes to get my permission to search the property. I wasn't about to give in now.

Letty smiled, revealing sparkling dentures. "And how is your dear Uncle Frederick today? I do hope he is feeling better."

"He's fine." I gritted my teeth. My 'dear' uncle was another of my big problems.

Letty giggled and fluffed her gray curls. "Well, you tell him that I'm going to bake my prize-winning cherry pie just for him. Now, I have to run into town for a while this morning, but I'll be back after lunch to comfort him in his hour of need."

I groaned inwardly. I did not need Uncle Frederick seducing this poor deluded woman. Aloud I said, "Mrs. Smith, I'm rather busy today. If you'll excuse me I have some work to do." I closed the door and locked it. I ignored the desperate knocking that ensued, along with the muffled, "But I didn't get any sugar!"

I turned around and faced my more immediate problem. Uncle Frederick sat at the kitchen table, poring over a very old book, a magnifying glass in his hand. He looked like Gargamel from the Smurfs, with his long black coat, bald head, and large beaked nose. He glanced up at me and sniffed. "You took long enough to get rid of her. But never mind that now. It's time to perform your incantation."

I had found the book in the attic when I first moved in and started going through Granny's belongings. The last thing I expected was a book of spells. Granny had never shown the slightest interest in magic in all my eighteen years of visiting her. I almost threw the blackened, shriveled thing away. Touching it made my fingers tingle. If it hadn't been for my great-grandmother's name (Samantha Rand McNally) on the inside flap, I would have burned it. Of course, now I wish I had.

My first spell had gone awry. My great-great-uncle (or so he claimed) had appeared in my living room in a cloud of smoke last fall, and he had been making my life miserable ever since. At first I had believed his claim that he was my great-grandmother's brother, Frederick, from New York. As time went on, I became less sure.

Uncle Frederick had pored over the book, exclaiming in delight. He had quickly realized that the spells wouldn't work for him. That had been a nasty day, with him ranting and railing about the perfidy of certain old women. Of course, he never blamed his lack of success on the fact that he was a second-rate magician with a small streak of magic and an even larger streak of malice. He knew all about the legend of the lost necklace, as well as a number of other tales about hidden or stolen jewels and gold. I suspected that he had been a jeweler's insurance agent before

I had pulled him from the past. When he discovered that I could actually work the spells, his eyes gleamed with greed.

"Get on with it, girl. It says here that the spell will only last an hour."

"But it's a waste of time. There is no treasure," I said.

He stood up, knocking the chair to the floor and towering over me. "Do you really think that line will work on me? I'm not some doddering old woman. Now begin!"

With trembling hands, I opened the book to the correct page, took a deep breath, and began to recite.

I never expected my spell to be so wildly successful.

I stared in open-mouthed wonder at the scene before my eyes. The far half of my modern kitchen had been replaced by half of a wooden cabin. A woman dressed in a white cap, a long, homespun gray dress, and a white apron, had her back to me as she stirred something on an iron woodstove. A sleeping baby was swaddled in an oval reed basket beside the stove. The man who had appeared by the table surprised me most of all.

He looked down at his hands as if he hadn't seen them for a couple of centuries. He was handsome in a dark, dangerous way: tall, muscular, and tanned, with a shock of straight black hair that hung to his collar and black stubble across his square jaw. If this were a movie, he would definitely have played the part of the criminal. He rubbed his hands down the front of his rough, homespun shirt. He looked up in amazement and smiled, which changed his threatening appearance to someone I could perhaps deal with.

"Glory be," he whispered. "I'm alive." He ran his fingers along the smooth skin on his neck. "It's as if it never happened."

The woman turned. She had curly red hair and a pretty face. When she saw the man, her face blanched. The spoon dropped from her hand and clattered on the floor. "Sean," she gasped.

The man turned and saw the woman for the first time. With a cry of joy, he sprang to her and crushed her to him. "Maggie!"

Then tears ran down her cheeks. "Oh, Sean. They told me you were dead."

"Do you think death could end my love for you?"

I've seen my share of romantic movies, but when he began to kiss her with a desperate passion that surpassed anything on the screen, I flushed and turned away from them. This was too private a moment for me to interrupt.

Just then Uncle Frederick seized me by the back of my neck and shook me. "Well, did it work? Is he there?"

What was I going to tell him? Even if the dark-haired man before me was a thief, he deserved better than to be in the clutches of this magician who, through my own ignorance and gullibility, had ensnared me and was now forcing me to do his work.

"Ah…y-yes," I stammered.

"Get on with it then," Uncle Frederick said. "Ask him where the necklace is."

I glanced over at the ardent couple and hesitated. I hated to break up their happy reunion.

Unfortunately, I was not free to choose my actions. Uncle Frederick shook me again, and the invisible band around my neck burned. "Well, girl, what are you waiting for?" His fingers sent a spark of energy down my spine. I winced. The pain was a reminder of what he was capable of doing.

I stalled for time. "Can't you see him?"

"Of course I can't. You're the one who did the spell. Now ask him. We haven't got all day."

I turned back to the little family. Sean had the baby in his arms. The love in his face as he looked at his wife and child took my breath away. Maggie was eagerly telling him all about their baby son, little Robbie.

I took a deep breath. "I'm sorry to bother you, sir."

Sean looked up and gasped. He seemed to see my half of the kitchen for the first time, and I saw his fear and amazement. He gave his wife the baby and pushed her behind him. His eyes darted around the kitchen. He snatched up the ax by the wood box and held it before him. "Who are you? What kind of deviltry is this?"

Uncle Frederick sent another painful jolt of energy down my spine. "He's just a common thief. There's no need to be polite."

After the magician had discovered what I could do, he spent months carefully researching and preparing for this moment. He forced me to begin practicing. Unfortunately, today would be the first in a long career of heists. I was his tool. I had been ever since last fall when I spoke that terrible spell that brought the mangy old man from out of the past. Oh, why couldn't I have left Granny's spell book alone?

I gulped and looked up at Sean. "Sir, could you please tell me where you've hidden the Montrose necklace?"

Sean's face hardened. "Is that what this is about? You've called me back from the grave to rob me? To deprive my wife and child of what they need to keep the farm?" Maggie, who huddled close behind him, regarded us in fear.

"I'm very sorry. I know this is a bad time, but I need the necklace."

Maggie looked up at him, worried. "Sean, please return their property to them and come home to me. Having you with me alive and well is worth more than all the money in the world. Somehow we'll manage."

His eyes narrowed as he studied me and my captor. "I am guessing that you have no choice in the matter?"

I shook my head.

A smile curved his lips. "The moth-eaten man holding you: he can't see or hear us, can he?"

Again I shook my head.

"What's he saying?" Uncle Frederick asked. "Don't try to double-cross me, girl."

I frantically tried to think of a way to warn the man without letting the magician know. "You commanded me to call up Sean McNally, but that was a common name of that time. I was just making sure he was actually the one who stole the necklace from the British lady. He's asking what year it is now."

"What difference does it make to him?"

"Well, a lot has changed in a couple of centuries. What if the place where he buried the treasure is covered with a building or a freeway?"

Sean's eyebrows went up. "What year is it?"

"2013."

Sean stared at me and whistled. "2013? Is that possible?" He rubbed his jaw as he looked around my kitchen. "You must be a powerful witch to have done this. What hold does he have on you?"

"Um." I shrugged and pointed to the band around my neck. It was a long story. I would have loved to tell him about it, but according to the magician, this spell would only last for an hour. If I didn't deliver, he would punish me. I shuddered, remembering the last time I had rebelled against him.

Sean set down the ax and kissed his wife. "It will be all right, love.

I'll deal with this. Wait for me here." He tenderly brushed the curls from her forehead.

She nodded. "I'll be here."

Then Sean turned to me and folded his arms. His eyes narrowed as he studied me. "Let's make an agreement, lass. I'll lead you to the necklace if you return me home alive to my family."

I nodded. "We only have an hour." I checked my watch. "Less, actually."

Uncle Frederick cuffed me. "What did I say about talking to him?"

Sean scowled at the magician. "That's no way to treat a girl, even if she is a witch." He went to the door of his cabin and opened it. Outside, he looked around in amazement. "A lot has changed, as you said. But I do know how many paces from my door it was." He began to count as he strode away to the east.

I was relieved that I had somehow brought the cabin as well as the people into the future. I had no idea why the spell had worked this way. I shrugged. As long as it worked, right? I tried to follow him, but the band on my neck tightened.

"Where do you think you're going?" the magician growled.

I choked as I grabbed at the band, futilely trying to loosen it. "He's leading us to the necklace," I croaked.

"Don't try anything, girl, or you'll be sorry you were ever born."

"Who me?" I squeaked. My uncle released me. The band loosened, and I gulped in large breaths of wonderful, fresh air.

Uncle Frederick snapped his fingers and a shovel appeared in his hand. He thrust it at me, and we headed outside. I looked to the left and right, but none of the neighbors were in sight. I was especially glad that Letty was gone.

Sean counted out fifteen paces east, which took us to the fence on the far edge of my backyard. Then he turned south and began to pace towards the thick stand of trees that grew at the back of my property. "Does he know about the old well?"

"No."

"What's he saying?" the magician asked.

I thought frantically. "He wants to know who owns the land."

Uncle Frederick swore and cuffed me again. "There's no need to converse with him. He's to lead you to the necklace, and then you will send him back to Hell. That's all."

I rubbed my aching ear. We walked into the woods.

Sean looked from the magician to me, and his mouth tightened in disapproval. "Don't worry, lass, I have a plan. Just follow my lead." We continued twenty-three more paces south, and then turned to the west where a tangle of ancient thorn bushes made it impossible to traverse.

Sean stopped, turned to me, and gestured at the bushes. "Is there something you could do?"

"What's the hold up?" Uncle Frederick asked.

I shrugged as if helpless. "He's going right through the thorn bushes."

"Do I have to do everything?" Frederick uttered a few words and pointed. The bushes yanked themselves out of the ground, flying to the left and right.

Sean raised an eyebrow. "I could have used that spell when I cleared this land. Nasty things, those thorns." He continued, counting ten paces west.

Sean stopped and turned around. "Wait a moment." He veered around something I couldn't see. "Tell him the necklace is in a box buried under a flat rock three paces ahead of him." He winked at me.

"Well, what are you waiting for?" Uncle Frederick snarled.

Sean held out a warning hand. "You must get him to step forward without you."

But how? I thought about everything I had learned about this greedy man these past months. I straightened up and pretended great confidence and disdain. "You're not really my uncle, are you?"

He swore. "What difference does it make?"

I folded my arms. "I want the truth."

The magician's face turned deep red. His eyes flashed in anger, but he nodded. "Very well. My fourth-great-grandfather, Douglas Reed, originally stole the necklace, but Sean McNally stole it from him. When Sean wouldn't divulge what he had done with it, Douglas made sure that Sean hanged."

Sean regarded him with interest. "I do see a certain resemblance to the original thief."

Frederick continued. "The legend about the necklace was passed down through the years to me. I put in long hours of research to determine the veracity of the story. I questioned McNally's descendants. I sifted through mountains of detritus from attics, yard sales, and antique shops. I performed certain magical tests. Finally, I discovered the truth:

84

your great-grandmother, Samantha, knew where the necklace was.

"I began to court her. I brought flowers to her and read her poetry. I even created a magical fireworks display one starry night. But the first time I mentioned the necklace, she became angry and threw me out. I went to her shop and offered to buy it. She refused. I threatened to expose her as a witch. She drove me away. I blackmailed her, but still she held out. Curse the woman. That necklace should have been mine years ago."

I scowled at Frederick. "So you're a thief and a liar, dogging our family down through the generations. I think I'll just keep the necklace for myself, and you can leave."

"After all I have taught you, you would pay me back by robbing me? I think not. Don't forget that I own you, girl." He pointed at me, and ropes of energy wrapped around my arms and legs.

I teetered and then dropped to the ground. "Ow," I gasped.

The magician picked up the shovel. "How much farther?"

"He says he buried the box only three paces forward, under a rock."

"Three paces forward," the magician muttered, standing in the exact spot I had just vacated.

"He has long legs. Long paces," I said helpfully.

Frederick gripped the shovel and lengthened his stride. "One, two, three–"

There was a sound of cracking wood. With a flailing of arms, Frederick fell into the earth, his horrible scream accompanied by the clanging of metal on brick. Abruptly the shriek was cut off. The net of energy that had held me disappeared. I scrambled to the large hole which now gaped in the loam and peered down into the inky darkness.

There was no sound from within.

"Is he ... dead?"

Sean nodded. "That well is fifteen feet deep. No one could survive that. Did I forget to mention that it was a dry well?" He grinned at me. "After a month of digging, my brother and I hit a stone shelf. We had to give up and start a new one further north." He pointed to the fountain in the center of my backyard. "You've done something artistic with it, I see."

I frowned at the rotted lumber fragments that surrounded the dry well. "It's a wonder someone hasn't fallen in before this." Of course, it had been hidden beneath all those thorn bushes. I wondered if Great-Granny Samantha had had something to do with that.

I sat up and rubbed my neck. The band of energy was gone. I sighed in relief. The magician really was dead. "I'm free."

Sean grinned at me. "What's your name, lass?"

"Molly McNally. Actually, I'm a descendant of yours."

He stared at me for a moment, then threw back his head and laughed. Still grinning, he took my hand with a firm, strong grip and pulled me to my feet. "Well now, that's grand. Sean McNally at your service. Come on then." He began to count as he walked away from me, dodging trees as he did so.

I skirted the gaping hole and followed him to another spot ten paces farther into the woods to the west. He squatted on the ground and dug his hands into the leafy compost. "That shovel would be handy right about now."

"Oh, right." I spoke a single word and snapped my fingers. The shovel appeared in my hand. I tried hard not to look at the blood on the blade.

Sean rolled a large rock to one side. He whistled cheerfully as he dug, sending up a heap of good, rich soil. "Just look at that earth. I always said this farm would be like the land of milk and honey. Two hundred acres of new opportunity: a chance for a poor Irishman to make a clean break and start life over. Has it brought you a good life?"

"Well, I inherited the place from my granny. Her husband's family lived here for generations. I think they all did fine." There was no need to mention that the house and its surrounding acre of trees and lawn were all that was left of the large farm that Sean had purchased after he came to America. In fact, I was glad that he didn't seem to hear the hum of traffic from the highway to the north. How could I explain modern transportation to him?

He laid the shovel down and reached into the hole he'd dug. He pulled out a rectangular object wrapped in leather so rotted that it fell away in shreds, revealing a small metal box. Sean brushed the dirt from it. His deft fingers pried off the lid. Then he removed an oilskin package. Within was something wrapped in a length of blackened cloth. He unfolded it and we both sucked in our breaths.

Sean's voice was reverent. "Time has not dulled its beauty."

I studied the necklace in his hands. The jewels appeared to be emeralds and diamonds, set in a delicate net of gold. It was truly exquisite, worth millions. "Wow."

"As you say."

"What will you do with it?"

He raised an eyebrow. "So you're not going to demand it of me?"

I shook my head. "That was the magician's idea. All I ever wanted was to learn a little magic."

"Believe it or not, I'm not a thief." He hesitated for a moment. "I was a young man, just off the ship from Ireland. I went to a stable, hoping for a job mucking stalls and filling water buckets until I could work my way up to exercise boy and then to racing. The stalls were full of the most beautiful horses you ever did see. Ah, lass, just stroking their heads filled me with dreams. The old man in charge of Winston Stables grinned at me and said, 'So you want a job here, do you? Tell you what. I've got me a game I'm late to. You sleep in the hayloft and keep watch over the horses tonight, and I will talk to Master Winston in the morning.'

"I had just blown out the lanterns and was about to go up to the hayloft, when a man came into the stable. He crept along until he came to the stall of my favorite, a big chestnut stallion. Now I didn't know anyone except the old man. This stranger could have had a legitimate reason for being there, so I waited and watched. He attempted to bridle the horse, but Gold Fire resisted him, rearing and squealing. When the man swore and raised a whip to strike Gold Fire across the head, I came to the rescue. With one blow I knocked the man to the ground. When I relit the lantern, I saw that a velvet bag had fallen from his vest. Curious, I had a look inside." He shook his head. "I was dazzled by the necklace. I'd never seen such wealth. By then the lights were coming on in the house, and the dogs were barking.

"Then the man awoke. When he saw the bag in my hands, he pointed at me and began to yell, 'Thief!' I panicked and ran. It turned out that these jewels belonged to the Lady Montrose, who had come from England to visit her sister, Mrs. Winston. I see by your face that you think I should have stayed and told them the truth. But who would they have believed: Sean McNally, an Irish immigrant, or Douglas Reed, the son of a high official in town? I feared to stay in Boston, so I went to my brother's farm.

"When I got my homestead claim, I buried the necklace, thinking that when the time was right, I would take it back and claim the reward. A few years later, Douglas somehow tracked me down. When I wouldn't tell him where I had buried the necklace, he accused me of the robbery and dragged me back to Boston to face the court. He had me sent to the gallows." Sean's fingers explored his unmarred neck. "How did you do it?"

I shrugged. Somehow I had pulled him out of the past just before his execution.

He looked off across the yard, deep in thought. "Lass, send me back alive and well so I can be with my family again, and I promise I'll make it right."

"You've got it." We shook hands once more. Somehow I thought that he would keep his word.

I frowned as I thought about how this might mess up the time line. "You might have to lie low for a while. I'm not sure what kind of repercussions this will have on your life."

"Whatever happens, I'll deal with it."

He refolded the cloth around the jewels and replaced them in the box, which he put inside his shirt. "So, what is it like here in your century?"

"It's a long story, and we've almost used up our hour." I grabbed the shovel and followed him back to the dry well.

He gestured. "I suggest you cover that with something. No need for anyone else to fall in."

"Right," I muttered. Another simple spell was all it took. The sides of the dry well collapsed, and a few moments later, all that was left was a mound of raw earth.

Sean shook his head. "You'll put honest men out of work with your spelling."

There was no time to examine my feelings of relief mixed with horror. Essentially, I had helped to kill a man and bury him on my land. Though he was evil and had kept me imprisoned in my own house since the fall, forcing me to do his bidding, the magician had taught me much. He wasn't from this time, so there was no one to notify. It was as if he'd never been here. Except my nosy neighbor, Letty, would surely wonder whatever happened to dear Uncle Frederick from New York. I sighed.

We returned to the house where Maggie sat in the rocking chair burping the baby. Sean held out his hand to her. "Come, my love, it's time we went home."

She smiled up at him with a look of adoration. "Wherever you are is home." They stood close together, fingers entwined, looking at each other with eager expressions.

I shook my head. What would it be like to love a man that much?

Sean turned to me. "Thank you. If we can ever do anything for you, we will."

"I think you already have. Good-bye and good luck."

A few words later, I was alone in my modern kitchen, and all was as it had been before I had made the spell, except for a lot of uprooted bushes in the backyard. I sank down in one of the kitchen chairs and took a deep breath. I hoped that everything had worked out for Sean and Maggie McNally. I would have to do some research and find out.

Anyway, I was free! I looked at the book of spells that sat on my kitchen table. "Granny," I said aloud. "I've learned my lesson. No more magic for me." I opened the top cupboard above the microwave and shoved the aged book in among my cookbooks.

I grabbed the broom and began to sweep the floor with determined briskness. From now on, I was going to be plain, ordinary Molly McNally, the inheritor of a country house and an antique shop. I would settle down, find a handsome man of my own, and have a couple of babies.

Even as I thought this, my fingers itched. Using the book had awakened something that had lain dormant within me, passed down through the generations. How long would I be able to resist its siren call? I thought about the dead magician, and my fingers tightened on the broom handle. One thing was for sure, there would be no more magic today!

The doorbell rang. I groaned. I yanked the door open, intent on imitating my gruff Granny. "Letty, I told you before that I'm..." All my words died in my mouth.

Standing on the steps, cap in hand, was the handsomest man I'd ever seen, with unruly chestnut hair, piercing blue eyes that were lit with humor, and a mouth that quirked upward. He was dressed plainly in workman's brown pants and a buttoned, off-white shirt with sleeves rolled up to the elbow, revealing muscular, tanned arms. I frowned. Somehow his clothing appeared to be straight out of the early nineteen hundreds. Those workman's boots, for instance...

"Sorry, but I'm not your Letty. Miss McNally?" I nodded mutely. "Davis O'Connell at your service." He gave me a bow. "Mrs. McNally sent me... to take care of the yard and whatever else you might need doing."

I stared at him, frantically trying to add up the pieces. "Mrs. McNally?"

"Samantha McNally."

I gasped. Had I messed up the timeline by sending Sean back alive?

I took a deep breath. Whatever. He was looking at me as if I was beautiful. "Oh, ah, yes," I stammered. "It just so happens that I do have some yard work. Some bushes. Um." I blushed. "Come on in. Welcome."

Perhaps the pie that Letty Smith would bring over later would come in handy after all.

I KNOW THINGS ABOUT TOILETS

Jeffery Bateman

Let's talk about our toilets, shall we? It's something we all have in common. Plus, I have some really good info to share that you'll want to record in that DIY book of knowledge in your head.

The porcelain throne. We sit on it, occasionally kneel before it, even hang from it in dire emergency, its cold surface providing the only measure of comfort we feel at certain times.

If you've ever repaired a toilet, you've probably bent over it, laid under it, maybe even done the Kama Sutra-inspired reverse sit technique while replacing the float mechanism. If you've replaced a toilet, you've wrestled gooey wax rings and rotted washers, and cleaned up stuff under the basin you shouldn't describe in polite company.

If you're a classic over-tightener, you've probably cracked at least one tank, entitling you to a free return trip to Lowes – "No Ma'am, I think it came like that…"

But I bet ya ain't done this:

After doing your "business," you pull up your sweat pants, only to hear an unfortunate plop as the Sharpie in your pocket falls into the bowl, right after you flush. We'll call this phenomenon: "The Sharpies! The Sharpies!"

Don't panic! You have 3 milliseconds to snatch the Sharpie from the bottom of the bowl before it starts to spin – but, you hesitate, 'cause, well, ewwww, and down goes Sharpie, down goes Sharpie!

You hope the Sharpie will go down vertically, but you know it won't. Sure enough, somewhere deep in the bowels (so to speak), of the toilet's base, your Sharpie wedges itself sideways but good.

Multiple hopeful flushes later, culminating in the dreaded over-the-rim bathroom floor deluge, you realize wishful thinking is not going to solve this one.

You break out the drain cleaning apparatus. You know, that corkscrew attached to a stiff cable with a crank at one end to make it twist in the pipe. You even have one for toilets specifically, 'cause, well, stuff happens.

This is where your PhD in blockage combat comes into play – right as you hit the serpentine at the bottom of the base. This is no mere sink trap! When you do, you're in the big leagues of man-portable drain cleaning systems. You jink up, down, right, left, repeat, until finally, you feel the head of the tool clear the bottom of the toilet. You're not sure what will happen to that Sharpie next, but at least it's going to leave your toilet, right?

Wrong. That Sharpie is wedged in there so tight the tool just keeps slipping past it. You discover this with your second flush test, helpless once again in the face of an unplanned waterfall event.

You drain, disconnect, and remove the toilet entirely, determined to get that Sharpie, come hell…and high water! So you jam the tool in the base again, this time from underneath – a sneak attack! You see the head of the tool emerge, just like the critter shooting out of the barnacle creature from Alien. Success! Time for another flush test! Third time's the charm?

When you go to buy your new toilet, may I recommend American Standard? That bad boy surges enough water into the bowl to raise a sunken ship, then sucks it down like a black hole. I don't believe the product of any natural process is capable of clogging it.

I don't know about Sharpies though. I'm no longer allowed to have them in my pockets.

NOTES FROM OWL BAR'S DIARY
Sundance, UT—April 26, 2015
Trish Hopkinson

I'd say I can call this home
though it's far from my birthplace—
this quiet human watering hole

often rests until afternoon,
when skiers wander in to get soaked
with their thirsty throats

and clunking boots,
bending an elbow
'til they're full as ticks.

All these flannel-mouthed folks
are fine enough, but don't hold
a candle to my outlaw roots.

My Irish oak first left Ireland
when Butch Cassidy sent for me
all those years ago. The gang
was good to me, kept me

oiled and in apple pie order.
I was just a shave tail then,
thought they'd never leave me,
but outlaws will be outlaws

and gunshots in Bolivia meant
I'd never see Butch again.

Time got away from me

and before I knew it, some
crazed biker joint gave me
a quick lick and a promise.

I stood helpless as a wallflower,
covered in shag carpet and
plastic countertop. I guess
you could say this place

saved me from certain death—
took me in, dressed me in my best
bib and tucker, polished up
each mirror and gave me
back my pride.

FLUFFY

Tim Keller

I don't hate animals, honest! Especially not dogs; what happened was just an accident. Plus it's not like they weren't aware; in spite of the myriad bites and barking tantrums, the nastier its disposition the cuter my employers seemed to find it. And why not? It's not like they had to take care of the thing; that duty fell to me, houseboy and glorified doggy butler.

Anyway, I was cleaning the upstairs bathroom…well, using then cleaning. I'm not really allowed in the master bath. Which as far as I'm concerned makes it all their fault. The life of a houseboy isn't as glam as you might think. They get the mansion, I get a closet, they get a full whirlpool bath, I get a sink and a toilet. You take your perks where you can get them.

The ferocious little throw rug was next to the tub just yipping away. Demanding another doggie treat, a walk, or maybe that ridiculous, rubber hotdog—who the hell knows? Fucking rat dogs; they're worse than babies. I mean, if a baby cries, you can always stuff a pacifier in its mouth and take a break, it's not like they can follow you, and even the most colicky kid will eventually tire itself out. Not so with Fluffy.

I had my earbuds in but nothing can shut out that high-pitched bark. Anyway, there I was doing my level best to ignore it like a game, you know? See how long I could ignore the little demon before finally breaking down.

I'd just finished dropping a deuce in the forbidden bowl, but the damn toilet wouldn't flush. Just sort of cleared its pipes a little, then nothing. Which was all I fucking needed! The one room I wasn't supposed to be in and I went and broke the thing. It's not like I could've blamed it on the dog, or that they'd believe me if I caught the thing in the act.

Well I'm no plumber, but what choice did I have? I lifted off the tank thingy and suddenly the dog went nuts, even for it. Except it was like, easier to ignore too, cuz I could see the problem, a brick jammed up against the ball thingy.

Praying the tank water at least was clean, I took the plunge, my hand anyway, but the brick was stuck. When it finally did come loose, I couldn't get it to lie down without blocking the flusher thingy.

I finally pulled the brick out to try another angle something, but the second it cleared the tank the rabid little son-of-bitch forfeited my game of 'Fluffy isn't here anymore' and sank its teeth into my ankle! And not just a nip, ya know? I was all kicking and shit, until I finally got in a good one that sent the demented little throw rug flying into the wall, but it turned and came at me again. What choice did I have but to throw the brick? Didn't hit it or anything, but suddenly there's all these pebble-things bouncing around the marble floor, and a broken baggie, still half taped to the brick.

Again—all their fault, all they had to say was "Stay out of the bathroom, cuz that's where we keep the meth, and I wouldn't have gone near it.

I considered my options: Flush it down the toilet, take a little, sell the rest and make a run for the border, or call the cops. I've watched enough Breaking Bad to realize none of these would work. *Or… I could get another baggie, and put everything back like I found it!*

I raced to pick up the toxic guilt pebbles, jamming them in my pocket as I went. That's when I turned for the baggie, and before I could even threaten the demonic little beast with a future in the window of a Vietnamese restaurant, it seized the baggie and made a break for the door. It was a short chase. Fluffy had turned away from the stairs and run into a dead end, where he stood his ground, fangs at the ready.

I opted for diplomacy. "Here Fluffy, good dog. Just drop the baggie, boy. Come on," I cooed. He stopped snarling, cocked his head, and allowed me to approach before making a break for it, but I caught him by that ridiculous cubic zirconia-studded collar and clamped his head against the floor with both hands.

Needle sharp teeth snapped impotently as I pried the spit-drenched baggie from his jaws—the empty baggie.

Now I'm no tweaker, but I've been clubbing long enough to

have learned a thing or two. A rock or bump of crystal is enough to get a grown man high, two is enough to send him on the adventure of his life. Three is definitely not advisable. By my conservative estimate, there were at least fifty bumps in the baggie. Which probably explained the deep gurgling snarls percolating up from behind me.

"Uh, Fluffy?" I coaxed.

A quick look at the hall clock confirmed I was out of time. Carl would be home in an hour, Jeff, soon thereafter. Dinner had yet to be started, and I was definitely going to have problems explaining why their beloved pet was performing selections from the live action version of Cujo.

"Hey boy," I said feebly, "how about a nice walk?"

Fur rose on his hackles as he roared—unsettling from a lion, petrifying from a Pomeranian. I barely had time to duck as he launched himself at my throat and out of the open, second-story window.

The silence from below told me everything I needed to know. Well, that and the thump.

☙

So ended my last job. No, I'd really rather you didn't call my former employers, I'm reasonably certain that wouldn't end well for either of us. At any rate, I can start right away; I just have one policy, no pets!

HUSH

Lorraine Jeffery

Blacks, republicans, immigrants all
Gays, Hispanics, liberals call.
Women conservatives, rich & poor
Educated, uneducated, all at our door.

You're stupid. I'm right. It's as easy as that.
We'll settle this argument. I'll grab a bat.

If we think differently then,
   he can't be our brother.
If we live one way then,
   he can't live another.

If we yell louder does it make us right?
Can we respect each other without a fight?

Nah!
You're stupid. I'm right. It's as easy as that.
We'll settle this argument. I'll grab a bat.

Hush our voices,
   Open our ears.
Listen with love,
   Don't magnify fears.

Each brings a different gift
   Do we need the strife?
Can't differences add to
   the quality of life?

Do we all have to look the same?
  Think the same?
  Talk the same,
  Act the same,
  Be the same?

This is America, not Russia or Greece.
Can't we just shut up and make our peace?

If we were quiet. What might we hear?
  Voices pleading,
  Hearts bleeding,
Differences fleeting?

Hush our voices,
  Open our ears.
Listen with love,
  Don't magnify fears.

PIPER

J. Anthony Gohier

Mathias gazed across the council chamber. The Governor stared back from the great stone chair at the other end. It was a throne really, but no one in town would call it that. It would be admitting too much.

"What do you want now, vagabond?" the Governor sneered.

"I have come for payment," Mathias answered.

"Payment? For what?"

The Governor coughed into his damp sleeve.

"The agreement was that I would be paid in full when the rats were gone."

"The agreement was that you would get rid of the rats. You played a flute."

"It's a pipe actually—and the rats *are* gone."

The Governor turned to the councilmen sitting around him in their wooden chairs.

"There have been no sightings since yesterday," the nearest said. "It would seem the rats have left."

"And the cause?" the Governor demanded.

"A shift in the climate, perhaps," said another councilman, "migrating predators."

"Or a disease," added a third.

The Governor shifted in his seat as he eyed the third man. "Then it has nothing to do with this man and his pipe?"

"Our sciences give no indication that music would have any effect on the rodent population," the Chief Councilman said.

"Well, there you are," the Governor said, waving a hand in Mathias's direction. "Still, let it not be said that the men of Hamlin are not fair in their dealings. Council, pay the piper."

The Chief Councilman drew a single coin from his pouch and tossed it at Mathias. It clattered on the stone and Mathias's feet.

"This was not the agreement," Mathias said.

"The agreement was for you to get rid of the rats," the Governor said, "not to lay about amusing yourself until they went away."

"There must be payment," Mathias said, "or there will be consequences."

"You have no power to threaten here, Pied-man, and you are no longer welcome in Hamlin."

The councilmen stood.

Mathias turned, leaving the coin on the floor, and left the chamber.

☙

An hour's walk outside of town brought Mathias to a clearing at the foot of the ancient mountain. Fireflies emerged among the trees and underbrush. A circle of stones rested in the middle of the clearing. The stones were weathered and cracked, and a few were missing, but wildflowers and toadstools had filled in the gaps.

Mathias placed his pipe to his lips and blew a solemn tune as he entered the circle. The mountain before him vanished and in its place stood a great stone hall, grown over with clinging vines. Mathias lowered his pipe. Auberon stood between the stone columns, glistening hair flowing back over his shoulders.

"You have arrived," the Great Sylph said.

"Empty handed, I'm afraid," Mathias replied.

"You bring no payment?" Cold light burned behind Auberon's eyes.

"The Governor refused. He seemed not to believe the magics had worked."

"The rodents fled the town, taking their pestilence with them, and drowned themselves in the sea. He can see that for himself."

"Unfortunately, sight does not always produce belief among mankind."

"And it is equally unfortunate for mankind that a lack of belief does not satisfy a contract. A boon was granted; payment must be made. It is the law you agreed to when you accepted our instrument."

"I know, Your Grace; I respect the laws."

The hall filled with whispers carried from the unseen realm beyond. Auberon looked away from Mathias, listening. Then the light in his eyes softened.

"Yes, Piper," he said, turning back, "you have always respected the magics. Our grievance is not with you, but with the people of Hamlin. Ease your mind. We shall settle the debt ourselves."

Mathias shifted where he stood.

"You have more to say?" Auberon asked, raising a silver eyebrow.

"Begging your pardon, Your Grace, but there are many people in Hamlin. I don't think they should all be punished for the actions of the Governor and his council."

"The Governor is empowered by the people. Regardless, we do not deal in punishments, only payments. When the sun is high tomorrow, we will exact payment from Hamlin."

"There are children in the town. They have suffered much already."

"We have heard your petition, piper. The laws must be answered."

Auberon faded, and the mountain appeared before Mathias again. He left the stone ring and wandered back down the foothills. Raising his pipe once more, he played a pensive tune as he looked for a tree to spend the night under.

❧

Sleep eluded Mathias. As the sun came up, he wandered the deer trails outside Hamlin. He clutched his pipe. He lifted it once—lungs filled with waiting notes—then silently lowered it again.

Cresting a low hill, he found a dark-haired girl sitting among the tall grass, a bouquet clutched in her small hands. She hummed softly to herself.

"Good morning, little one," Mathias said, strolling to her side. "You are young to be out on your own."

"I always gather the morning blossoms," the girl said. "Mother says they help with the smells."

"Your mother will be pleased," Mathias said. "But she'll worry if you're gone long."

"I know; I just needed a rest." The girl pulled a short crutch from among the grasses and pushed herself up from the side of the hill.

Tucking the crutch under her arm, she shambled toward the town, one leg hanging limply beneath her.

"You have a kind heart," Mathias said, though she had moved too far to hear him.

The girl's humming resumed, keeping time with her wobbling gait. Mathias raised his pipe again and mimicked the girl's tune. She turned back and listened for a few measures. Then she smiled at him and continued toward the town. Mathias blew a long low note, and then the tune shifted.

He thought of the other children in Hamlin, who were probably waking now. He thought of those who had shivered in their beds while the rats plagued the streets. He thought of those who had watched their mothers and fathers cough out their last breaths. He thought of those who still cowered in the shadows, hungry eyes pleading with all who passed them. His pipe sang somber and dark, then paused as the girl reached the edge of the town.

"It would be better if you were not in Hamlin today."

Mathias blew through the pipe once more and a new tune rolled and bounced along the breeze. The girl stopped to listen again. This time her smile began slowly and spread until her whole face shone. A minute later, a boy wandered from the town and stopped next to her. As her smile spread to his face, another boy joined them.

The flowers dropped from the girl's hand as she turned her crutch and began ambling back toward Mathias. The boys followed and quickly overtook her. More children emerged from the town, and the crowd pressed toward him.

Mathias turned and walked back into the hills as he continued his tune, filling each note with laughter his heart didn't feel. He let his feet wander, heading nowhere in particular, just away. The children thronged around him, their laughter fluttering through the trees.

☙

The tree line broke and the mountain rose before them. Mathias paused, staring briefly at the stone circle, and then turned back.

"Mathias."

The tune caught in Mathias's pipe. Auberon stood in the circle.

"We heard you playing," the Great Sylph said.

The children hung back at the edge of the clearing as Mathias lowered his pipe. "I used the magics, I know. I will make their payment."

"Yes," Auberon said. "This will suffice."

106

Mathias furrowed his brow. "What will suffice?"

"There are many ways these children can serve us, and we will watch over them. Hamlin's debt is paid."

"That's not –" Mathias began, but Auberon looked past him to the edge of the clearing.

"Come children," Auberon said, raising his arms and taking a step backward. The tune Mathias had played surged from the mountain and beyond, carried by hundreds of unseen voices. Smiles returned to the children's faces and they ran forward. One by one they vanished into the stone circle at Auberon's feet.

When they were gone, Auberon lowered his arms and looked back at Mathias. The song continued to ring through the air. Mathias stared back, his pipe hanging limply in his hands.

"Fine," Mathias said, "you have your payment. Leave Hamlin in peace."

"There are more," Auberon said.

"What?"

Auberon nodded toward the trees. Mathias turned. The dark-haired girl still struggled toward them, her crutch sliding and snagging along the path. Behind her, two boys crouched and clung to each other. One of them stared at Auberon with wide eyes. The other angled his ear toward the mountain, his eyes looking at nothing.

"Their infirmities slowed their pace," Auberon said, "but we will tend to them."

"Leave them," Mathias said turning back to Auberon.

"We will mend their ailments," Auberon said. "In our country they will see and hear and walk."

"And there will be three more broken hearts in Hamlin. Your payment is satisfied. Leave these."

Auberon's head tilted as he listened to the voices carried from beyond the mountain, and then his deep eyes stared into Mathias's heart. "The payment is accepted." And stepping forward into the ring of stones, Auberon was gone. The song died on the winds.

Mathias turned back toward the trees and found the dark-haired girl just entering the clearing. A few wavering steps brought her to his side.

"Please," she said, "I want to go too."

"And what of your mother?"

"Please, I want to go."

Mathias looked into her eyes. "I don't know if I have saved you or condemned you, little one," he said. His hands tightened around the pipe. "Take the others. Return home."

❧

It was three days before hunger drove Mathias back to civilization. He had wandered as far as he could from Hamlin, but he could not outrun the winds, or the memories they carried. He didn't know the name of the town he had stumbled across, but he found his way to an inn boasting a sign of a black kettle over its door. He sat at a table in a dark corner, painfully aware that his purse was as empty as his stomach. The last coin he had seen had been left on the floor of the council chambers of Hamlin.

One hand rested on the pipe strapped to his belt. He had thrown it away once, but it found its way back to him. Magics weren't that easy to be rid of, he was as much their instrument as the pipe now. He should have known better anyway. You can't fool the magics. He had learned that long before he accepted the blessing of the Great Sylph. He leaned back against the wall, his hood pulled low over his closed eyes, and listened to the crowd.

Most of the talk was trivial—young men boasting of various exploits, older men complaining about their wives, and elderly men complaining about everything else. A lad whose voice had barely broken mooned over an unrequited love. Dull and hardly likely to pay well. And too young to understand what he was bargaining with. A group of bearded men grumbled over corrupt officials. Tempting, but likely to attract more attention than he needed, at least until he had better motivation than an empty stomach. A merchant ranted to his underlings about highwaymen that had raided his caravans and made off with—his daughter. Mathias eyed the merchant. He was obviously well fed, and his cronies didn't appear to be starving either. Perhaps he could stand to see what magics would bring him if he had the disposition for it. And Mathias would need a hearty meal to face the will of the magics again himself.

Mathias approached the table. "You have a problem," he said.

"Who are you?" the merchant demanded, glaring at him, "Militia? Mercenary?"

"Just a man with a knack for solving problems."

"And you think you can solve mine?"

Mathias's finger traced one of the pipe's tone holes. "I can," he said, "for a price."

108

NEXT YEAR

Amanda Luzzader

We almost died. All of us—the entire human race. It was a pandemic that took the world's population from eight billion to just ninety-two million in a little under three years. I don't remember being sick. No one does, because the serum that is keeping us alive also wipes away our memories.

Some things are still there. We know how to talk and walk and eat. I can read just fine. Do math. I know what roses, cats, and roller coasters are, even if I'm not sure I've ever seen them before. What's missing are events, experiences, people. It's like waking up in a different place than where you went to bed, only to realize you didn't exist before you fell asleep—I wrote that in my first journal. Everyone gets a nice new journal each time. "Write every day," the officials say. "Leave nothing out." You get one year. Just one year before you have to take the shot again, and you forget all over.

I live with my son, Arie. I only know he is my son because the health department sent us both to the same house in year one. We found some photo albums, but only knew for sure when we found his birth certificate. I started laughing when I realized I had a teenager, and then we hugged, and we've been together ever since. I only know because I wrote it in the journals.

Eve lives with us, too. Who knows where she came from. We found her sitting on the dead grass in front of our house with that dazed, bewildered look everyone has when they first reawaken, but no one had taken her to a house. Maybe it was burned in the riots. She didn't even know her name, so eventually she named herself: Eve—the first woman, at least she thought so. Even though I'd guess she's at least twenty years older than me, Eve's my best friend now. We even share a bed, and then Arie's in the room down the hall.

Earlier this year, Eve came down for dinner and stood in front of the table where Arie and I were eating canned meat. The meal was cold, but at least it wasn't rancid.

"I want to ask you something." Eve clutched her journal in her front of her chest.

"What is it?" I asked.

"I—I was thinking, what if I took that day out from my journal. You know, that day at the market?"

Eve had heard about this place—the market—where you could trade things for food. It was kind of shady sounding, and definitely unofficial. She thought we could trade the pistol we'd found in the bedroom closet and get enough to eat for a month. Arie told her it was too dangerous, and I agreed, but Eve must have felt she had to do it, seeing as we had taken her in and all when food was already so scarce. She went by herself without telling us.

There was a bad man there. He not only took the gun from Eve, but he beat and raped her, too. We found her—bruised and bloody—in the middle of a street. She couldn't even talk for a couple weeks. She wakes up in the night screaming. I try to calm her down, but it's almost like she can't even hear me. There are other things—she's lost weight, she's jumpy, she doesn't like to leave our house. Sometimes, for no apparent reason, her whole body will start to shake. Eve's not the same.

"I mean, do I really need to record everything?" Eve asked. "Do I have to remember what happened?" Yellow splotches still colored her skin where the bruises were the worst. "If I don't write it down, then next year I won't know. It'll be like it never happened. The nightmares can finally end. Do you think it'd be okay?"

"I don't know," I said. It had never occurred to me to not record what happened each day, especially the big things. I started wondering whether I, myself, had left things out of my journals in years past. As the authors of our own stories, could we really believe the things we'd written? Could we trust our own records? I couldn't blame Eve for not wanting to remember.

"I think it'd be all right," I told her.

"But it wouldn't be the truth," Arie said. "It happened whether you write about it or not. And it's in our journals, too. You can't change what happened. I'm very sorry, but you're a different person because of it, and if you don't keep some memory of it, the person you are now will cease to exist."

Eve's face reddened. "I don't want to be the person I am now! My life's a living hell, and I'm tired of being scared all the time." Her knuckles turned white as she clutched the journal even tighter. "I'm sorry, but I'd rather die than have to remember." Tears ran down her cheeks.

"Oh, Eve." I wrapped my arms around her as she sobbed. "It's okay. You don't have to."

"Go ahead and take it out." Arie stood and threw his napkin on the table. "It's not like the journals allow us to really remember anyway. They're just words. We all know that."

As Arie climbed the stairs to his room, Eve took a deep breath and opened the book on the table. She flipped to the offending pages and tore them out.

We were both quiet as she lit a candle. Its cinnamon fragrance and smoke filled the air as she held the papers over the flame. The pages blackened and curled before falling to ash, the darkness spreading across the paper until it nearly reached her fingertips, and then she shook the glow out and dropped the remnants to the floor.

"It will be better next year," Eve said.

❧

Knowing what a sunset is and experiencing a sunset are very different things. That's one good thing about forgetting—you get to do things for the first time again. Arie must have still been upset because he didn't join me on the rooftop to watch the sun as it sunk below the horizon.

We write in our journals things we need to remember—what people say, projects we're working on, where things are located, medical items—but Arie and I try to record other things, too. Like the sunsets, because even though it happens every day, it's never quite the same. Arie writes beautiful descriptions of them. I just try to ingrain them in my mind—burn them into my memory—so the haze can't take it away. My gut tells me there's got to be some way to remember. But then again, I said the same thing in journals one through five.

I've heard there's some people—rich people—that have other people following them around videoing everything they do or taking pictures so a synopsis of their year can be compiled. Maybe it's just a myth. To be honest, I don't even know anyone that has electricity.

But when I'm watching the sunsets, I take out this old digital camera I found—the battery's long dead—but I'll hold it up and push the button like I'm snapping a picture. Just in case it helps—a mental picture, if you will.

Maybe we'll remember next year. That gets said as much as "God bless you" or even "Goodbye." Maybe we'll remember next year. The scientists, we're told, are constantly working on the formula—desperate to remove the side effect, but I suppose it's hard for them when even they forget who they are each year. "Write it down," they say. "Write everything down. Everything." I'm on my sixth journal now; one for each year.

After the day's light extinguished and the stars began to appear, I climbed back into the house through a window. None of the windows had glass anymore. I peeked into Arie's room. I couldn't see him in the already darkened room, but I could sense he was there.

"Don't be upset with Eve," I said. "She's gone through so much."

"It's not her I'm upset with," Arie said.

As my eyes adjusted to the dark, I could see him lying in his bed staring at the ceiling.

"What is it?" I sat on the corner of his bed.

"Everything. I mean, what's the point of doing anything if we're not going to remember? Falling in love? Having a family? Building a life? How can we know who we are, if we don't even know who we've been? And writing it down—what a joke. Like you could love someone just because it says you do in some book."

I looked down at my hands. "It's worked all right for us."

Arie sighed. "I mean romantic love. Do you think something written in a journal could even come close to actually experiencing those things? And that's assuming we can even believe the things that are written there. It's like we die every year. We're not the same people; we don't exist anymore, but we keep on living. That's what's important, right? Whoever we are ceases to exist, but we don't die. This may have started as a plague, but it's the zombie apocalypse now. We are the living dead."

When he grew silent, I reached for his hand in the darkness, and when I found it, I squeezed it tight.

"Maybe we'll remember next year," I told him.

He was quiet then. Too quiet. I suddenly realized my hands were trembling. "Arie. You mustn't give up hope. Look on the bright side of things. We're alive, aren't we? We've survived."

"Maybe forgetting is the blessing," Arie said flatly. "Maybe forgetting all the shit and misery is the bright side."

"Don't say that."

He rolled over to his side, his back facing me. "I'm very tired," he said.

I couldn't remember what it was that a mother was supposed to do. Tears brimmed in my eyes. "Things will get better," I said as I walked to the door. "You'll see."

∾

It was three weeks and four days later when I found him hanging from the upstairs banister with a belt around his neck. I only remember reaching my hands through the bars of the stairs and trying to pull him up and hearing the desperate screams that came from the depths of my soul.

Where the other people came from, I don't know. They pried my hands off from him, pushed me into a bedroom. But I could still hear my screams.

Later, when I knelt beside the banister and fingered the marks on the wood, Eve found me and sat next to me.

"He was already gone," she said. "You couldn't have saved him."

And Eve was right. I'd lost him not that night but weeks before. I tried to make him see that it didn't matter that we couldn't remember, it only mattered that we lived. But he couldn't see it that way. For him, it was an empty world with empty dreams.

It didn't make sense the way I loved Arie. But I did. He was my son, my everything. I felt real physical pain when he was gone, like my heart was quaking, on the verge of bursting open and I wished it would so at least the pain would stop.

I trudged through the next weeks. Eating was a challenge. Getting out of bed a chore.

"You don't have to keep all this pain," Eve told me. "Soon you can forget it all."

She told me to change my journals—to take Arie out. Start the year as a new person. A new woman. One who wasn't stuck in sadness. "You can be whoever you want to be," she said. "Just change it."

I read through everything I'd written since year one. My eyes swelled from crying so much. After I'd read it all, I took a pen and turned to the first blank page. There was something important I had to write because I knew I'd never forget. I held the pen steadily and pressed firmly. I had a lot to say, and it started with:

I am a mother. My son's name is Arie.

TOO SOON FOR GUNS

Chadd VanZanten

I don't know where Glen got the idea I would ever want to go pheasant hunting, least of all now. It's maybe because six years ago I said something like, "I love pheasant hunting." I maybe said that. Thing is, he never listened to a word I said back then, so it's not really my fault.

And even if he was listening, Glen had to know I said it because I was engaged to his daughter at the time. Deanne loved me to death, of course, but I had to work much harder to impress Glen and Helen and the others, so I said lots of stupid things—everyone knows you don't listen to anything the fiancé says. The fiancé is the most pathetic suck-up you'll ever meet. Back then if Glen said, "Ray, let's you and me get undressed and cuddle awhile," I'd have unbuttoned my shirt and said, "Glen, that's just what I was thinking."

I never won him over entirely. Not like the other brothers-in-law did. Deanne and me didn't go to church and never had kids. We moved away for school. The other brothers-in-law were churchgoing farm boys who stayed put and wore their hair short. When they said they loved pheasant hunting, by God they meant it.

That's why I've spent a lot of time wondering where I stand with Glen and Helen now that Deanne's gone. One of the first things Glen said to me after she died was, "I do not want you blaming yourself for this."

It was a nice thing to say. It really was. But it was impossible to keep myself from thinking he was lying. Because there's so much guilt and blame after a car accident. So, I'd go over his exact words—"I do not want you blaming yourself for this." He never said it wasn't my fault,

115

he just said he didn't want me blaming myself. So, should I anyway? He didn't want me to, but did he blame me?

With Helen, things were a lot easier. As soon as she showed up for the funeral, she appointed herself my handler and official spokesperson. When I'd shut down, she'd step in. Like when I'd sit and dwell on some stupid thing for thirty minutes, an hour. I thought a lot about the ambulance for some reason—how it was so grimy and old. Most ambulances are immaculate, brand new. Deanne's was in real bad shape. I'd sit thinking about what something like that means, and when one of the brothers-in-law would come over and tell me it was time for supper, I'd just go right on thinking. That's when Helen would materialize, pat my back and say, "Let's go ahead and leave Ray be. I don't think he's hungry right now."

And Glen actually did try to absolve me, in his way, but I just couldn't trust him. He told me I should come stay with them for week after the funeral. I told me I'd stay two, just to see if he'd try and back out. He didn't. In fact, out of nowhere, he started calling me "son" all the time. He never did that before, and I could tell he had a hard time getting used to it. He'd tack it on where it didn't fit, like maybe Helen put him up to it.

He'd say, "If you use that downstairs toilet, you gotta jiggle the handle after you flush. Son."

Staying at Glen and Helen's was hardest in the evenings, after dinner. The house would get so quiet. Glen and Helen wouldn't say hardly anything. Even the presence of their dead daughter's husband in the house couldn't break up their quiet dishwashing collaboration, their TV schedule.

When the news was over, I'd go down into the basement and get in Deanne's old bed. Helen had no compunction about bunking me there.

"Small," she said, "but it's still a good bed. You can toss those stuffed animals on the floor. I'll put 'em back later."

A sodium arc lamp stayed on all night somewhere among Glen's outbuildings, casting a shaft of light through Deanne's basement window like a stationary moonbeam. It lit up Deanne's little study desk and her ancient computer. Pearl Jam poster on the paneled wall. Taped to the mirror above the dresser were clippings from the local paper about her at the state track finals long ago. In the dimness, I could just make out her newsprint face and I looked at it each night until I fell asleep.

Mornings were a little better. I'd get up late and Helen would have breakfast ready. We'd talk about things we might do, like take a trip together, the three of us. Then I'd go back to bed. Glen didn't like that, so after a few days he made me come with him while he walked his dog Nixon.

"If you felt up to it," Glen said one morning, "you could help me do a brake job on that truck."

"Yeah," I yawned, shrugging, pocketing my hands against the chill. "I could hand you the wrench."

He laid a bunch of other plans that we never carried out—a shed that needed painting, fruit trees that needed pruning. He even suggested we drive into Billings and check out the Custer monument, but I know for a fact nothing was ever said about pheasant hunting.

Because I don't love pheasant hunting. Technically, it's not even fair for me to say I don't like it because I have never been pheasant hunting. I once answered "yes" when the brothers-in-law asked me, "do you want to go pheasant hunting?" and I spent time in their company while they shot up some pheasants. I think when I was in scouts I may have even fired a shotgun to get ready to hunt pheasant at some future time. But I've never actually posed a threat to any pheasant.

Glen didn't care about any of that. He never really asked me if I wanted to go.

As we sat down for some of Helen's pecan waffles he asked me, "You up for all day?"

"Yeah," I said. "Sure. I guess."

"Good," he said, nodding. "After we eat we'll go out and see if we can't shoot a couple pheasants. Son."

I looked up from the waffles, wondering if it was a good idea to go someplace remote with Glen while he had a gun on him.

"No hurry," he said. "Whenever you're finished. It'll be good for us."

I looked around for Helen. She took her appointed station at my side and patted me on the back. I waited for her to say, "Oh Glen, Ray doesn't want to do that today."

But she didn't, and unless I was partially blind with grief, I'm pretty sure I saw her give Glen a little nod before she turned and went into the kitchen.

The only other woman in the room was Mrs. Butterworth, so I stared at her awhile. She was no help. She stood next to my plate, hands clasped across her generous, transparent waist, with an expression that seemed to ask, "Will there be anything else?"

I went to Deanne's bedroom and looked through my suitcases for something warm enough to wear. All I had was a black hoodie. I got dressed then sat on the bed, listening to Glen thumping around in his study.

"Where did you put that green shoulder bag? Helen? Did you move it?"

"You put all that stuff in the garage," she called back.

Soon Glen knocked on the door. I opened it from where I sat on the bed. Glen stood in the doorway in this wool coat and cap. He looked around inside but didn't come in. As if some barrier were still in place there, one that I was audacious enough to cross but not him. I stood up and he turned and I followed him to his study. He produced a key and opened a gun locker.

"Twenty gage, twelve gage." He pointed to each gun. "Four-ten, another twelve gage, and that one's a twenty-eight. These birds'll flush long. Pick your poison."

I didn't know if I should put some thought into my decision, or if I'd even been given enough information to choose. There was a time when I knew what the numbers meant, but I couldn't ask for a refresher now. In a few more minutes the woodstove heat of the house would melt Glen in his coat and hat. He looked at his watch. Twelve gage shotguns were the only kind I had any experience with at all, but I assumed picking one of them was too easy, childish maybe. I considered the others but had already forgotten which was which.

Glen chose one of the twelve-gage guns, the pump-action kind. Then he pulled open a drawer in the bottom of the locker and sorted through the ammunition there.

"You know," I said, "maybe I'll just tag along. I don't even have a current hunting license right now." This was true, but I had never had a hunting license at any time.

"We can get you one at the filling station," he said. He picked up the other twelve gage, a double-barreled Winchester, and handed it to me. "Here. Just take that one."

A half hour later I was zoning out in Glen's Chevy as we drove into the pasturelands on the edge of town. The mist had retreated and the autumn landscape glowed with a coppery tint. After a while Glen slowed and pulled the truck off the road.

"We're here," said Glen, thunking the truck into park.

"We're where?" I said.

"Here," he said, lifting a finger to point out the windshield. "This is it."

We looked out on a series of cropped hay fields lying in the sun like vast hemp doormats.

"Yeah," I said. "Looks great."

We got out of the truck. Nixon hopped down from the bed and stuck his nose in the dirt. Glen came around and put a box of Remington shells on the fender.

"That enough for starters?" he asked. "You a good shot?"

"Oh, I'm sure I'm a little rusty," I chuckled.

Glen loaded his shotgun and then worked the pump to chamber a shell. He shoved a few shells in his pockets, and then stood looking at me.

"Shells?" he asked.

"Right."

I took two shells from the box, but couldn't open the gun with them in my hand, so I put them back. One fell out and rolled down the fender. I flinched to catch it but Glen snagged it first. He put it in the box and then took hold of my shotgun barrel, which I had allowed to swing in his direction until it was aimed at his groin. I apologized and pointed the gun at the ground. Then I realized I didn't know how to load the gun at all, so I turned and tilted it blindly.

"This is a lot different than what I'm used to," I said. Over the trigger housing there was a brass oval etched with a pheasant in flight. "Wow, Glen, this is a really nice gun. You sure you want me messing with it?"

"Here," said Glen. He thumbed a lever situated in plain sight between the two barrels, and the gun fell open by the breach.

"Right, okay," I said. "For some reason I thought that was the safety."

Glen walked out into the morning. He whistled up Nixon, who snuffled down the edge of the field.

I inserted a shell in each barrel, closed the breach, and the gun fired, blasting my father-in-law square in the ass.

Glen spun about and took one halting step, as though he thought he might walk it off. Then he collapsed stiffly into the hay stubble.

I dropped the gun and ran to him. Nixon barked at me ferociously, lunging, teeth clacking. Glen's face was drawn into a terrible grimace, his lines and wrinkles tight and pale. I pulled off my hoodie to put under his head, babbling something I couldn't hear over Nixon's barking.

"Nixy," roared Glen. "Enough. Sit."

The dog quieted down, and so did I. Nixon turned in a circle and sat, licking his chops in a pathetic, jittery way. Then we both sat quietly, awaiting further instructions.

Glen's voice went to a sort of low buzz. "Ray," he said.

"Yeah Glen."

"You shot me in the ass."

"I know I did. I am so sorry."

"Wasn't your fault," he said, waving his hand. "It was too soon for guns, maybe."

"Maybe. Yeah."

"Ray."

"Yeah Glen."

"Wasn't your fault," he said, and he looked me in the face.

"I appreciate that, Glen." I got my hoodie bunched up under his head. Then I took out my phone and dialed.

"Ray."

"Yah. Glen."

"I'm going to pass out."

"You're probably going into shock."

"Doesn't hardly surprise me. Been awhile since anybody shot me."

I nodded at him and talked to the dispatcher. "You're going to be fine, Glen."

"Yeah," he said. "I expect we both'll be."